FED UP WITH LUNCH

FED UP WITH LUNCH

LUNCH

HOW ONE ANONYMOUS TEACHER REVEALED
THE TRUTH ABOUT SCHOOL LUNCHES—AND
HOW WE CAN CHANGE THEM!

SARAH WU

CHRONICLE BOOKS

SAN FRANCISCO

Library of Congress Cataloging-in-Publication Data:

Wu, Sarah.

Fed up with lunch : how one anonymous teacher revealed the truth about school lunches—and how we can change them! / Sarah Wu.

p. cm.

ISBN 978-1-4521-0228-3 (hardback)

1. National school lunch program—Case studies. 2. School children—Food—United States—Case studies. 3. Children—Nutrition—United States—Case studies. I. Title.

LB3479.U6W8 2011

371.7'16—dc23

2011018136

Manufactured in the United States of America

Designed by Jennifer Tolo Pierce

10 9 8 7 6 5 4 3 2 1

Chronicle Books LLC
680 Second Street
San Francisco, California 94107
www.chroniclebooks.com

For Charlie, my son;
for my students, my inspiration; and
for lunch ladies everywhere, who work diligently
to feed millions of hungry kids.

Contents

Note: Names have been changed to protect the identity of private citizens. Ironically, Mrs. Q can now reveal herself!

Introduction

The most difficult thing is the decision to act, the rest is merely tenacity. The fears are paper tigers. You can do anything you decide to do . . . the process is its own reward.

—AMELIA EARHART

In my five-year career as a teacher at a large elementary school in Chicago, I had rarely set foot in the cafeteria. In fact, I hadn't eaten a school lunch since eleventh grade. Why would I pay for school lunch when I could bring exactly what I wanted from home? But one fateful morning in October 2009, I was running late, trying to get Charlie, my noncompliant toddler, dressed. Pushing his feet into his little shoes and stuffing him into his fleece jacket while he attempted to squirm out of my grasp, I realized that I hadn't packed my lunch. *No big deal,* I thought as I successfully got him out the door. *There's a cafeteria at school. I'll buy lunch there.*

I had no idea that eating one school lunch would dramatically change the course of my life.

That day, for three dollars, I purchased the only school lunch available: a bagel dog, a Jell-O cup, six Tater Tots, and chocolate milk.

The bagel dog (a hot dog encased in soggy dough) came in a plastic package. Tough on the outside and mushy on the inside, it was like no bagel I had ever tasted. The hot dog was bland, not juicy. The wimpy Tater Tots (which counted as that day's federally mandated vegetable) were pale and wilted in my mouth. Instead of a piece of fresh fruit, like the crunchy apple I would have packed if I'd had time that day, I was given a few cubes of pear suspended in bright red Jell-O.

I was starving and needed fuel to stay energized for my students, so I ate the meal, choking down as much of the mushy bread as I could stomach. But I couldn't believe that this was the kind of food my students were being served, especially knowing that most of them came from low-income families and that this was probably their most substantial meal of the day.

I have worked as a speech pathologist in Chicago Public Schools District 299 for the past five years. Most speech pathologists rotate among schools, but I am assigned primarily to one elementary school with an enrollment of around 1,300 students from preschool to sixth grade. The student population includes a lot of English-language learners from families that speak Spanish, Ethiopian, and Burmese. There are African American students and Caucasian students, too. My school serves a community of people mostly living below the poverty line; the number of children eating free and reduced lunches is well over 90 percent. These students need and deserve fresh food to help them succeed in life. Even more than mine does, their bodies demand decent nourishment from school lunches. If more people knew about the pathetic quality of food in public schools, and—at least in my district—the limited amount of time kids have to eat their lunches, surely more people would want to do something about it.

That lunch made me mad.

Anger can be an ugly emotion. I recognize its importance under the right circumstances, but when I see an angry person, my first reaction is, *Whoa, what's wrong with him?* The way I see it, getting mad represents a loss of control—and that's not me. Nevertheless, I felt a deep anger bubbling up whenever I thought about the students at my school eating that processed and crummy school lunch. I felt compelled to do something. I considered starting a boycott or staging a protest, but what could one teacher in a cash-strapped district really do? Realistically, I was already putting all of my energy into providing a quality education for my students and, when I arrived home, my family got whatever was left over. Did I have enough fight in me after a typical day to become a school lunch activist?

This question stuck with me (much like the bagel dog, or maybe it was the Tater Tots, that had me quietly burping my way through that memorable afternoon). Was there some way to channel my outrage about these lunches in a positive way? Picketing and organizing are great for some people, but what about a more subtle and persistent campaign to raise awareness and encourage change? Sometimes, doing something in a quiet way can have powerful results.

When I was developing my annual goals for 2010, it hit me: I would buy my lunch every school day in 2010 and blog about it. I already had a personal blog that I updated on a monthly basis. It was tiny—an online journal that I shared with just two readers: my mother and my sister. With a schedule that already felt packed, attempting to write a daily blog post for a wider audience seemed overwhelming. But maybe it was worth a try.

Was I qualified to blog about school lunches? I debated with myself about this for weeks. Speech pathology is a health science, which made me acutely aware of the health status of my students. To earn my master's degree, I had taken lots of science courses and I had a basic understanding of physiology, especially as it relates to the speech and hearing mechanism. My biology training certainly didn't make me a nurse or a nutritionist, but I could appreciate the mind-body connection. Treating your body right is critical to maintaining your voice, your speech, and your brain. And perhaps even more important, as a teacher and a parent I was deeply invested in the health and well-being of young people.

My plan was simple and straightforward: I would help to raise awareness about school lunches by eating them. I felt that my perspective as an educator working inside a school was unique—and hoped that other people would be interested (but not *too* curious because I had a job to hold down and didn't want to draw attention to myself as a whistleblower).

When I told my husband about my idea, he laughed and said, "Forget it. We have enough on our plate as it is. Not to mention what would happen to your health."

Initially, I agreed to drop it because working as an educator in an elementary school and being the mother of an active toddler is challenging enough; I didn't need the additional time commitment that blogging would entail.

Also, I hate to admit this, I was afraid.

I'm not a subversive person. I was an obedient child and never even went through a rebellious teenage phase. Maybe that's because I wore braces the entire four years of high school, which was not conducive to coolness or boyfriends. Because of my parents' employment situation, I moved all over the country while young. Being "the new girl" every other year made me wary of making waves. While I thought it was unlikely that more than a handful of people would stumble across my blog on the Internet, it still felt risky to expose myself, my school, and my district to public scrutiny. I was a chicken happy to stay on my private little perch.

But during the next few weeks, whenever my students seemed particularly sluggish in the early afternoon, or complained of tummy aches after lunch, my fantasy about starting a blog returned. I considered how hard the teachers worked to reach their students, and how difficult it was for the children to focus when they came back from their painfully short twenty-minute lunch breaks. When I gathered small groups of kids for speech class after lunch, I noticed more than one student staring off into space for a few seconds, their eyes glazing over. I would see one of them with neon red blotches on her white shirt—she had eaten the red frozen juice bar, but had she had enough time to eat the remainder of her lunch?

I wondered if any researchers had looked into the connection between inadequate school lunches and academic performance. And I wondered if parents and the general public knew what the schools are feeding kids. Sure, the parents might be receiving monthly menus, but the descriptive power of plain text pales in comparison to the grim reality of school food. The colorful names of the entrées put a very optimistic spin on the food-like items that the children are consuming on a daily basis.

I resolved once again to go forward with my idea. And this time, I didn't check with my husband.

The blog Fed Up With Lunch: The School Lunch Project started in January of 2010, chronicling each meal I ate with my thoughts about the experience and a photo or two.

I created an alias for myself: Mrs. Q. Being anonymous would allow me to be creative with the blog without putting my career on the line. My family relies on my income combined with my husband's salary to pay the bills. I didn't want to get fired, even though I wasn't sure there would be much of a case against me—since what the kids eat every day isn't proprietary information. Still, I worried about impacting the education of my students if I blogged using my real name. My anonymity protected me, as well as my school and school district, from being harassed in real life. I didn't want anyone I worked with to find out I was keeping a public record of the school lunches the kids and I ate. I was determined to work my normal schedule— to do my job, buy school lunch, photograph it, eat it, and then go back to the work I loved. I realized I could take a picture with my cell phone, send it to Blogger, compose a basic blog post, and publish it all in less than five minutes. I managed to do all of the blogging and tweeting outside of school hours.

A year of eating school lunch: The idea doesn't sound that radical, but Fed Up With Lunch turned out to be transformative for me. It pushed me from private citizen to public advocate. It changed my family's relationship with food for the better. The project made people from all over our country, some who had never considered it before, think about school lunch. I'm grateful to the generous, passionate, and well-informed people who stumbled upon my blog and took the time to share their views and opinions. My blog posts and their comments reverberated as I became more aware of food politics than ever before. A community of parents, teachers, nutritionists, lunch ladies, and foodies sprang up around Fed Up With Lunch ready to exchange thoughts and ideas about school lunch, education, and the state of children's food in America. I knew very little before, but now I can say that food is a whole lot more important to growing children than I thought.

I thought I had no power when I started my blog, but I still wanted to make a difference in my own quiet way. I had no idea it would create an uproar, a rallying cry, and ultimately a community for those of us who knew, or were just discovering, that school lunch reform is vital. It didn't hurt that at the same time I was launching my blog project, Michelle Obama was making childhood obesity and school lunch reform a topic of national concern with her Let's Move! campaign, and Jamie Oliver had just launched his reality show *Food Revolution,* about school food and its link to obesity and poor health.

By eating these school lunches, I just hoped to raise awareness about school food for a few parents, teachers, nutritionists, and foodies. Amazingly, my blog soon became the poster child for school lunch reform. My school lunch photos were part of the national zeitgeist. I was a chicken nugget on the school lunch tray of life.

The last section of this book, Mrs. Q's Guide to Quiet Revolution, explains how you can get involved. It may sound corny, but just like Margaret Mead said, "Never doubt that a small group of thoughtful, committed citizens can change the world. Indeed, it's the only thing that ever has." If enough of us band together, there's a real chance that we can change the current quality of school food in neighborhoods all over this country. And wouldn't that be a wonderful thing?

CHAPTER 1

Mrs. Q Goes Undercover
(Like a Beef Patty Masquerading as Meatloaf)

The value of identity of course is that so often with it comes purpose.
—RICHARD GRANT

When I started my blog, it was important for me to remain anonymous. I revealed the lunch I ate every day but kept many details to myself. Being anonymous was fun, scary, and sometimes frustrating when I wanted to say more but was afraid to give too many clues that might blow my cover. At this point, finally revealing myself to you as the real Mrs. Q comes as a big relief for me. It's been increasingly hard to hide who I really am with people I care about—and I care about my students and coworkers, the lunch ladies at my school, and, of course, the remarkable group of caring people who have followed and contributed to my blog.

So allow me to introduce myself. I am Sarah. Or as I'm known at school: Mrs. Wu. How did I brainstorm my alter ego: Mrs. Q? The name came to me as an alias simply because it rhymes with my last name! See? I was hiding in plain sight all along.

MY SPEECH ROOM IS ON THE SECOND FLOOR of the largest elementary school I have ever seen, spanning the length of one city block. Haugan Elementary looms large with three floors of classrooms. The cafeteria is on the first floor and, to accommodate a student body of approximately 1,300 students, lunches are divided into five lunch periods. To get down to the cafeteria from my room, I have to walk approximately sixty feet along the corridor of the second floor and then down a massive stairway that opens out to a foyer in front of the cafeteria. The foyer fills up with students with the ebb and flow of scheduled lunchtimes.

On January 4, 2010, my mission began. I was ready to put my stomach on the line to make a point about school lunch. Like putting on an invisible cloak, I assumed my role as Mrs. Q and marched down to the cafeteria, nervously clutching the three dollar bills I would use to pay for my food. Having correct change is required when buying school lunch: Lunch ladies are not in the business of making change for the usual twenty-dollar bill I keep in my wallet. Feeling like a character in one of John Le Carré's spy novels, I greeted the lunchroom manager, Pearl, with a confident smile as I stood in the foyer with lines of students streaming past. Pearl positioned herself in front of the lunch line talking to teachers and students. I told her as I handed over my cash, "I'll be eating a lot of school lunches this year because it's quicker than packing my lunch. I . . . " I was about to say more, but she was called away to attend to something in the kitchen. I was happy I was cut off because when you're undercover, it's best to stick as close to the truth as you can. It keeps you from slipping up and my intention was not to lie to anyone. What I said was true—it would be easier to come to school and buy lunch instead of taking the time to prepare and bring my own midday meals. That was the one big advantage of eating school lunch every day, given how much work was involved in getting myself and my toddler into the car in the morning—not to mention waking up my cranky, sleepyhead spouse.

On the day of my first school lunch for the project, pasta with meat sauce was the main dish. Glancing at the long lines of children waiting to pick up their food, I picked up my already-filled tray and hurried out of the cafeteria. Bursting with adrenaline, I glanced back like an inexperienced thief leaving a crime scene.

Each weekday, as I climbed up the massive staircase clutching my tray, I thought one of two things: *What have I gotten myself into?* and *Please don't hate me forever, Pearl!*

I hustled back to my room, set the tray on my desk, and carefully arranged the items for maximum visibility for a cell-phone camera shot: pasta with meat sauce in a little heated box covered in plastic, green beans in a smaller disposable container, a breadstick, chocolate milk, and a blue raspberry "icee" thing that resembled a popsicle without the stick. Was that supposed to be a serving of a fruit?

Glancing at the door to make sure no one was watching, I pulled out my cell phone and took a couple of pictures. Then, tucking the phone back in my purse, I settled down to eat. My utensil—a spork—came wrapped in plastic that also held a little, bitty napkin and a straw. Fascinating. Even though the main course had very little pasta and a lot of meat sauce, it actually became one of my favorite meals. And during the next few weeks, after some meals that were seriously hard to choke down, I came to appreciate that first pasta dish more and more.

AFTER A FEW DAYS OF EATING SCHOOL LUNCHES, I confessed to my husband, Mike, what I had been up to. Mike summed up his view on my project: "As soon as it stops being fun, don't do it anymore." I thought that was a funny thing to say, because it really wasn't very fun, even from the start. It was nerve-racking, exhausting, and a huge gamble. Mike didn't view the blog like that at all. At first he just wanted to make sure it didn't reveal our true identities (check! I was anonymous). And then, his only remaining concern was how I would fit the blog into our schedule. I told him, "It only takes a few minutes to cell phone blog, sweetie. It's not a huge deal."

When the project began, it was quick and easy. Blogging in secret was no big deal: Other teachers knew I was busy, so eating in my room didn't raise any eyebrows. Stealthily carrying lunch up to my classroom, taking a quick picture, and blogging about my school lunch into the night was thrilling and exhausting. I became a master actress: It had to look like I was really excited about buying the food because why else would I be eating school lunch every day? Compartmentalizing was critical for maintaining my anonymity; I didn't think about my blog at work and when I was at home working on the blog, I didn't think about my job as an educator.

Two weeks into January, I came home from work and noticed that I had twenty comments on a blog post. I put my hands over my mouth and yelled out for my husband, "Come and look at this!" A young, savvy nutritionist-in-training named Andy Bellatti had tweeted about my blog, and this tweet had come to the attention of Marion Nestle, a leading nutritionist in New York, who wrote a related blog post on her site. She shared my blog's URL with all of her readers. I had no idea how many people came to visit Fed Up With Lunch: The School Lunch Project that day, as I had not installed any program to track daily hits. This thing was already getting bigger than I'd expected.

On the last day of January I installed a hit tracker and realized that after just one month, I was getting about one thousand hits per day. I was truly shocked, excited, and terrified. I confided in my husband, "I'm feeling so bad about doing this, like I'm betraying all the lunch ladies at school." I had great timing: Mike and I were trying to get our son ready for bed and Charlie was squirming out of his pajamas. I should have waited to share that with my husband, but I let myself worry out loud. "I care about everyone I work with. What if they hate me after all this comes out? Worse, what if I lose my job?"

Mike knew how to calm me down. After assuring me that the blog would not get me fired, he reminded me, "If it's not fun, just stop." I tried to continue along with his line of reasoning. It *was* only a blog, right? I could take it on and make it work and find time by organizing myself better. I could reach out to readers if I had questions about blogging or school lunch regulations.

This blogging thing is no big deal, I tried to tell myself, *This is going to blow over.*

I KNOW THAT AT SOME POINT IN YOUR life you ate hot lunch at school. It might have been pretty good, like a grilled cheese sandwich and commercial tomato soup that kept you warm on a cold winter day (that is still one of my favorite combos at home). Or it might have been bad—like unrecognizable turkey bits swimming in salty gravy over soggy toast. In either case, I have news for you: School lunch has gotten worse. *Much worse.*

Every day, I watched small kids in the cinderblock hallway outside of the lunchroom holding laminated lunch tickets with their names written in dark permanent marker. Usually the little kids were jumpy and hungry, fumbling with large plastic lunch trays. I thought it was cute when the little kids caught sight of the bigger kids in the line opposite theirs. It was like they couldn't believe their luck: They would be eating at school just like the big kids.

In the cafeteria, I heard the lunch ladies say, "Keep moving, and take one of each." Small children tried to balance their trays while scanning the lunch line. Frequent menu items at my school included chicken nuggets, hot dogs, pizza, pasta, and hamburgers. Fast food. In fact, chances were good that those of my students whose parents worked for Taco Bell, McDonald's, Starbucks, and Subway would get similar food when their parents brought home leftovers from their jobs.

I wondered what kids who went through the line for the first time thought about the food being encased in paper and plastic. Because of their exposure to fast food, I imagined that they weren't as put off by the enormous amount of packaging as many of the readers of my blog have been. Certainly, after a week, they were fully indoctrinated and not fazed at all.

The kids pushed forward in the lunch line as cartons were stacked neatly on their trays. A lunchroom aide led them to the picnic-style table where the class sat down. The smaller kids couldn't start eating yet because they weren't able to open any of the lunch containers, including the little bag with the spork. They waited and fidgeted until it was finally their turn for help. *Wham, wham, wham.* A lunch aide moved down the rows, stabbing a spork through the plastic covering of each parcel of chicken nuggets just like she was going down an assembly line.

The school where I work only allows twenty minutes for lunch—including lining up time. I know it had to be shocking for the students who just started school to learn that there was no time to eat. They sat down with their food and suddenly it was time to clean up. There was no time to try the veggies, which were often Tater Tots, or even to open the fruit cups. The kids got up slowly as a lunchroom worker dumped their trays into the trash. Due to food-safety regulations, food could not be saved for later.

The way the big kids moved through the line was almost entirely different. Many were quiet, but others formed small circles around friends, eagerly anticipating the one break in the day when they could socialize. (There is no recess at my school. Another story altogether—I'll have more to say about this in a later chapter.)

Sometimes the older kids' faces were expressionless as they filed through the lunch line, taking each of the mandatory components of the lunch and placing them with a *thud* onto their trays. They left the line and passed a garbage can. Occasionally, kids took their entire lunches—planned out so thoughtfully by the USDA—and dumped them right into the trash. Usually the chocolate milk was spared and downed quickly. These kids had seen every menu item a thousand times, they didn't like the food, and if they didn't eat, they could spend lunchtime chatting with friends. Having no recess, when else could they relax? As somebody who values lunch and a break in the middle of the day to relax and socialize with coworkers, it was hard for me to witness this.

Kids Say the Darndest Things　　DAY 11

The frozen fruit-juice bar, which I called a fruit "icee" on the blog, was on the menu for the first time. Most of the time, the lunch offerings never contained nutritional facts or ingredients, but sometimes the prepackaged, factory-made products did. The label said that it was supposed to be a "cherry" frozen juice bar, but when I looked at the ingredients, I found out that it contained high-fructose corn syrup as well as Red #40 and Blue #1. Food colorings are often made with synthetic dyes, including Red #40, Yellow #5, Yellow #6, and Blue #1. Research in Europe has revealed that artificial food dyes cause hyperactivity in children.

The Icee was very sweet, as in puckering my lips. I sucked down a few sips and then stopped. It was too sweet for me to finish. Later, I talked to a couple students about the meal. They said they liked it. I asked if they ate everything and one student said he didn't eat the green beans.

The main meal was pasta and it was served with a stiff, prepackaged breadstick made of white flour to satisfy the USDA's requirement for grains, which often leads to the inclusion of two wheat products in every meal. Both of the kids didn't eat the breadsticks because they were "too busy talking" and ran out of time. Can't say that I blame them!

The lack of time for healthy social interaction was only the beginning of the problem. My school was on probation for one year for failing to make adequate yearly progress (AYP), which is required by the No Child Left Behind (NCLB) Act. When a school isn't meeting standards and the children are failing to understand basic concepts, I think every rock needs to be overturned to search for the cause. Certainly parents and teachers play huge roles. But when a school is failing, school-based nutrition should be examined, too. Instructional quality is absolutely tied to students' performance, but what about the effects of the high quantity of sugar, sodium, fillers, and food dyes in these processed school lunches? After lunch, I routinely observed glazed-over looks and frequent sleepiness in my students. How could I successfully reach them after they had eaten so much sugar?

Studies have shown that children who suffer from poor nutrition during the brain's most formative years score much lower on tests for vocabulary, reading comprehension, arithmetic, and general knowledge.[1] Additionally, even moderate undernutrition (inadequate or suboptimal nutrient intake) can have lasting effects and compromise cognitive development and school performance.[2] In my work, I have to justify everything I do as it relates to the state learning standards. Oddly, the school lunch program has no ties with the Department of Education, as it is wholly under the jurisdiction of the United States Department of Agriculture (USDA).

The National School Lunch Program (NSLP) was established in part as a way for the USDA to find a market for surplus commodity foods. In 1946, when the National School Lunch Act was signed into law by President Truman, it was a perfect marriage: The USDA had the extra food and children were hungry. To me in 2011, it seems a bit odd that any part of a student's educational day would be governed by the USDA. Some have said that maybe the USDA should get out of the business of school lunches and let the Department of Education run the show. I'm not sure that's the answer, but I would love to see education incorporated into the cafeteria because I believe that school lunch may be one of the most important things in any student's day, as it relates to learning.

One might think that the problem of "bad" school lunch is restricted exclusively to low-income and urban areas. But thanks to a number of conversations I've had on my blog with parents and educators around the country, I have learned that the food I ate all year is the same exact food served in many schools across this country, regardless of district funding. It should be noted that there are some excellent school lunches served in this country and these can be found in both urban and rural settings. But even some of the best-funded schools serve food that is not nutritionally the best for children's needs. However, kids from these homes are able to compensate by eating healthful breakfasts and dinners because they have increased access to fresh food at home. Kids living in homes that are below the poverty line don't always have the ability to eat better at home. The Centers for Disease Control define food deserts as areas that lack access to affordable fruits, vegetables, whole grains, low-fat milk, and other foods that make up the full range of a healthful diet; according to a 2009 study, such food deserts exist in the United States.[3] My school, for example, is within walking distance of McDonald's, but a drive is required to reach a grocery store with fresh, healthful food.

Returning to my room from the cafeteria each day, I passed hundreds of students waiting in line for their food. They looked at me and waved or they checked out what was on my tray. Every single time I saw their faces, I was reminded of why I had decided to eat school lunch just like they did, every day. Many of them come from homes where money is scarce and they get excited about lunch, even when they don't know what it is they are about to eat. For some of these students, the only food they got to eat was what they had at school. In a survey of teachers by Share Our Strength, a national nonprofit dedicated to ending childhood hunger in America, 86 percent of teachers reported that many of their students come to school hungry, and 65 percent said that most kids rely on school meals as their primary source of nutrition.[4]

If we want to give them a fighting chance at life, we need to give them good food at school so that they can learn new things and become the best they can be. They also need to know that fresh food is important to the health of their bodies and their minds.

Free and Reduced Meals

To qualify for free lunch, students' families must have incomes at or below 130 percent of the poverty level. Children are eligible for reduced-price lunches when their families' incomes fall between 130 percent and 185 percent of the poverty level. "Reduced price" means that the students cannot be charged more than forty cents per lunch. (According to the USDA, from July 1, 2010, through June 30, 2011, 130 percent of the poverty level was an annual household income of $28,665 for a family of four; 185 percent was $40,793.)[5]

CHAPTER 2

Do You Want Guilt with That?

- - - - - - - - - -

If all difficulties were known at the outset of a long journey,
most of us would never start out at all.

—DAN RATHER

Taking photos of chicken nuggets was not something I ever thought I would be doing. But there I was, covertly running to my classroom, closing the door, and taking quick pictures of bizarre foodstuffs. My cell-phone camera made it easy to snap a picture. I found myself whispering to the nuggets, "Hey, get ready to be viewed by thousands of people on the Internet! Who knew you would get so famous when you left the factory?" Sometimes I ate them plain and sometimes I slathered them with barbecue sauce. It depended on whether or not I needed to lubricate the dry pellets on their voyage down to my stomach.

I noticed bursts of comments and activity on the blog, and then it would die down. With every fit and start, I would wonder why I did this in the first place. It took me hours of work every night to perfect each blog post and to return every e-mail. People were taken with the blog, which made me nervous, but then I would chuckle. With every tiny panic attack came a period of relief and, ultimately, personal growth. Even though I was new to the blogging world, and mostly just a hack, I liked blogging. It was fun to share my viewpoint with readers and addicting to read their comments. Little by little I became more comfortable being Mrs. Q. I started taking my martinis shaken not stirred.

I DON'T REMEMBER EVER EATING CHICKEN NUGGETS at school or at home as a child. My mother was a free spirit who met my father in Australia when she traveled across the world to be an art teacher; she believed in eating granola and prunes. But thanks to my school lunch project, I consumed 133 chicken nuggets in one calendar year, which seems to me like a lifetime supply. The kids love them, but I find them boring and tasteless—similar to gruel. I'd always assumed that chicken nuggets were fried pieces of plain chicken breast meat. I guess those food scientists had me fooled; chicken nuggets are only about 50 percent chicken.[6] Most of the ingredients are modified corn bits (cornstarch, corn fillers, dextrose, emulsifiers). I couldn't find a list of ingredients for the chicken nuggets I ate at school, but I did find the list of ingredients in a Chicken McNugget. McDonald's states in advertising that it uses "all white meat chicken," but they don't say what else is in those nuggets:

> Chicken, water, salt, sodium phosphates. Battered and breaded with: bleached wheat flour, water, wheat flour, food starch-modified, salt, spices, wheat gluten, paprika, dextrose, yeast, garlic powder, partially hydrogenated soybean oil, and cottonseed oil with mono- and diglycerides, leavening (sodium acid pyrophosphate, baking

soda, ammonium bicarbonate, monocalcium phosphate), and natural flavor (plant source) with extractives of paprika. Prepared in vegetable oil (canola oil, corn oil, soybean oil, and hydrogenated soybean oil) with TBHQ and citric acid added to preserve freshness. Dimethyl-polysiloxane added as an antifoaming agent.[7]

I'm pretty disturbed by that ingredient list. To think that my students and I ingested something similar to that on a semiregular basis in 2010 is really upsetting. What *did* I eat again? Was it food?

Ingredient lists are closely guarded by the food corporations, including Sodexo, Aramark, Chartwells-Thompson, and Preferred Meal Systems, that provide the meals for school lunches. Like any spy worth her salt, I tried to research what was in the food we were eating, but there are no full-disclosure labels on chicken nuggets. I checked online, on the lunch menus, and I looked for anything posted at my school. I came up empty. In my distict, no teacher or parent can see the fillers that make up so much of the food eaten in the school cafeteria. To me, an outside observer, it appeared that companies were afraid of ingredient transparency. I wondered what, if anything, they were trying to hide from parents, teachers, and school administrators. When I did further research, I found some alarming statistics about antibiotics. According to the Food and Drug Administration (FDA), twenty-nine million pounds of antibiotics were given to livestock in the United States in 2009, accounting for 70 percent of all antibiotics used in the country annually. [8] You'd be hard pressed to see "antibiotics" listed on any label under "nutritional information."

Adults can check ingredients on packaging when they are shopping at the supermarket to stay informed about what is going into their bodies. But parents looking at school menus don't have this option. Perhaps the ingredients in school lunches are not available to parents because the cost of the paper on which they would be printed would be prohibitive. Parents reviewing the monthly menu may presume that the nuggets are unprocessed chunks of chicken or something at least more palatable than a nugget containing less than 50 percent chicken. The main ingredient in chicken nuggets is what I affectionately call "chicken foam," or some derivative of mechanically separated chicken. I Googled the picture and found something that looked disturbingly similar to strawberry soft-serve ice cream coming out of a machine.[9] It alarmed me. That's chicken!? What part?

As the months wore on, I started to notice the abundance of processed chicken: popcorn chicken, chicken nuggets, and chicken patties. Identical beef patties had different names including hamburger, Salisbury steak, and meatloaf. After three months I felt physically revolted. I was getting tired all the time, and the lunches almost never left me satisfied, but I was determined to stay true to my original goal.

Kids Say the Darndest Things   DAY 31

The rib-b-que sandwich was offered to the students. I asked one of my students, "What did you have for lunch today?" and he replied, "A hamburger." I found that the cafeteria served many different processed hamburger meat products, but that the kids were not fooled by fancy names on the menu ("meatloaf," "rib-b-que," etc.). When they got a "hamburger," they knew it.

My adrenaline peaked each day as I surreptitiously scurried from the cafeteria back up to my room, scanning to see which teachers might have noticed me in the hallway. I never ducked into the threshold of another classroom to escape attention, but occasionally I'd hustle to get to my room as quickly as possible. I needed to take a picture of the lunch in private. I didn't eat with the kids because it would have been too hard for me to take a picture of the lunch with the jostling of little bodies and the prying eyes of the lunchroom monitors. Walking or running back to my room, I tried to avoid invitations to eat lunch with coworkers. I needed to take a picture of the lunch in private.

Sometimes it felt lonely to eat by myself every day. If I really needed companionship over lunch, I would tell a friend, "I need to run to my room to get my water bottle." I would hurriedly snap a picture of the school lunch in my room, and then take my lunch to the teachers' lounge.

Just so it's clear, let me repeat that I was not screwing around with my cell phone all day. The only time during the school day that I even thought about blogging was during my twenty-minute lunch period. But I was confronted with food issues as they related to student performance pretty much every day, and I couldn't help thinking about it now and then. During my teeny tiny lunch break, I took a quick picture, scarfed down my food, and often had five minutes left over to do some required paperwork at my desk. Those lunches were designed to be eaten quickly and they met that goal.

I longed for a sandwich. Just a plain sandwich from home. One day, as I was walking to the cafeteria, I noticed a lot of kids carrying lunch boxes or bags to the cafeteria. It struck me as peculiar. At my school, the amount of children eating free and reduced meals is well over 90 percent, so seeing the majority of students with lunches from home was an anomaly. Looking around, it seemed like it was the big kids who were packing lunch that day. *Hmm, interesting.* I shrugged and entered the cafeteria. "Today we have peanut butter and jelly," the lunch lady announced with a tight thin-lipped smile. Looking down at what was on my tray I thought immediately of a foil-wrapped ice cream sandwich. And I had two. I paid, said thanks, and went on back to my room.

Something was wrong with my sandwiches: They weren't on bread. Where bread was supposed to be was a graham cracker–like substance, which had been previously frozen and was crumbling as it thawed. The peanut butter and jelly was about an inch thick. Gag. The bonus of having packaging on this main entrée was that ingredients and calories were listed. Each peanut and jelly bar (it did not deserve the generous label of "sandwich") contained three hundred calories of weirdness.

I couldn't eat more than a couple of bites. They were vile and strange. The kids with the packed lunches should have warned me! That night when I got home, I was sick. I couldn't get up off of the floor of the bathroom for a couple hours. I was physically decimated, but as soon as I felt better, I blogged everything. My husband said to stop when it was no longer fun. The evening in the bathroom was no picnic, but I had no intention of abandoning my mission. Without meaning to, I had turned into a cell-phone journalist and that was new ground for me. When I was in fifth grade, I wanted to be a journalist and work with Dan Rather. Suddenly, here I was, a reporter on the front lines, filing commentary from the field.

CHICKEN NUGGETS MAKE REGULAR APPEARANCES on school lunch menus but they also have a starring role on children's menus at restaurants. Kids love chicken nuggets. I like going out to eat and especially enjoy Thai, Japanese, and Indian cuisines. I can't tell you the number of times that my family will sit down in a restaurant known for healthful fresh food and find chicken nuggets on the separate kids' menu. Why can't kids eat what adults do? Maybe the appeal is that chicken nuggets are easy to eat: You can grab them in one hand without silverware and take a bite. Unlike other food, nuggets offer one uniform texture: no surprise when you take a bite.

When children are learning to eat, each texture and taste is new to their mouths and it's all about experimentation. Every parent has a picture of a kid with baby food all over his/her face; it's a fun time. Some kids are excited by the new food, but others are hesitant to explore and prefer to stick with what they know. Chicken nuggets are never going to offer something sensory to kids who don't want to explore.

While I could dare parents to abandon chicken nuggets and take the time to be purposeful in offering healthful foods at home, I have a confession to make: My son ate chicken nuggets at day care. It's not something I'm proud of, especially after I learned more about them. Pink chicken-nugget foam is not something that I want my kid to eat on a regular basis. Actually, I'd prefer it if most children and adults avoided nuggets. My kid didn't know any better when he got them at day care and neither did I. Thanks to the well-informed followers of my blog who were kind enough to set me straight, I learned so much about chicken nuggets and real food that I stopped letting him eat the day care's chicken nuggets. In fact, I ended up packing him his own food, including snacks, so that he could avoid not just processed food but also canned fruit and vegetables, since most cans are lined with bisphenol A (BPA).[10] I didn't want to be thought of as a helicopter mom, but then again I didn't want my son to eat diced carrots with a side of bisphenol A.

IN FEBRUARY I STARTED GETTING INTERVIEW REQUESTS every couple of days. I was overwhelmed by them, and I felt forced to come up with a standard reply: "Thanks for contacting me. I'm not interested in conducting any more interviews because I am concerned about my employment. Please check back with me in a few months as it's possible I may feel differently after I have gotten further into the project." Every interview request brought with it another paranoid thought. *How did they find the blog? Who do they know? Will tomorrow be the day I get hauled into the principal's office?* I didn't want to blow off the interview requests entirely because I didn't know if there would be a time when I would feel more comfortable granting them to a small group of people. I didn't want to be rude, but I knew I wasn't ready to talk to anyone at that time. It felt too soon and a little too scary.

I was getting so much out of my interactions with the followers of my blog, but I wasn't ready for prime time. I was not a school lunch expert yet; I was more like a student, cramming for a surprise quiz every day.

CHAPTER 3

Pizza with a Side of Paranoia

You better cut the pizza in four pieces,
because I'm not hungry enough to eat six.
—YOGI BERRA

In March, three months into my yearlong challenge, I looked over the school calendar and realized that there would be a huge gaping hole in lunch blog posts: spring break. Every school district had a different spring break and anyone with even limited investigative skills would have been able to determine which school district didn't have class. I decided it would be best if officially I continued eating school lunch every day, but instead of posting them every day I would delay their posting by a day and instead substitute a different food-related post. I wanted to have content for those days, but I didn't have time to write it all myself, so I asked my readers if any teachers, students, food service directors, or administrators would be interested in eating school lunch and writing guest blog posts. I was flooded with volunteers.

It was great to have so many experts giving different points of view and sharing their stories. I was learning a lot, but oftentimes I felt overwhelmed. One of my followers, a lunch lady named Ali, contacted me to say that she was inspired to start her own blog, Brave New Lunch. By reading her blog, I found out that some school pizzas have sixty-two ingredients![11]

My readers were curious about the lunches. Why did it seem like some lunches offered a lot of grains, but others didn't? I headed over to the USDA's Web site.[12] I searched, clicked, read, and then searched, clicked, and read again. Reading a Greek phone book would have been an easier task.

Looking at the lunches I ate and comparing them to the USDA regulations I found online, I learned that a small container of fries counted as a vegetable. Potatoes are a vegetable but aren't they a starch too? The fruit requirement could be satisfied by a small cup of fruit juice, which meant a loss of soluble fiber from the flesh of the fruit. The gooey processed cheese from a sandwich was considered a meat alternative. Popcorn chicken was a meat, but even with all that breading, it wasn't a grain. I know nutritionists are involved in meal planning, but this "kid-friendly" stuff was taken to an extreme—and it was all legal, according to the USDA.

One of the more interesting things I found was that two servings of grains are generally required per meal. Do you think of pizza as a grain? According to the USDA's requirements for grains, a piece of school pizza counts as not one but two servings of grain because it is measured in grams of "creditable grains."[13] That's quite the stretch, considering that rice only counts as one serving. Yes, rice—one of the most widely consumed grains on our planet—is wimpy compared to school pizza. In addition, the cheese on pizza counts as a serving of "meatless substitute." This means that one slice of pizza supposedly meets the students' daily protein and grain requirements. The cheese on the pizzas that I ate didn't seem substantial enough to be a true, filling protein. Still, whatever—the kids ate it up, right?

School pizza is usually served once a week. But it's not the school pizza that you and I remember from our childhoods. You know the kind that came off of massive baking sheets served by sweet lunch ladies with hairnets? That's what I remember from high school. That pizza wasn't half bad. Today more than 90 percent of food brought into cafeterias is frozen, including the pizza. And the pizza at my school comes in its own little box. How Lean Cuisine!

You might ask, "So what if kids eat frozen pizza at school?"

I don't think medical science has gotten to the point that they know what consuming a list of fillers a half page in length does to a person's body, especially the developing bodies and brains of children. Unfortunately for many children, school is the best chance they get to eat fresh food, and instead they are getting sixty-two-ingredient pizza.

"We serve what the kids want to eat" is the standard comeback from nutrition directors to parents and teachers who question why fast food is on the menu at school. Sure, a kid likes pizza, but can't we make it with fewer ingredients? Wouldn't it be cheaper to use fewer than ten ingredients? And why not throw a couple veggies on those pizzas?

Some argue that it makes sense for schools to offer foods children would choose to eat on their own. The argument is that if children want to eat the food, then we've got a better chance of filling their bellies—and of converting kids who pack into kids who pay. We might ask ourselves: Is it better that they eat a plate full of french fries for lunch than throw away a salad? Better questions: How can we get kids to eat the veggies? How can we offer fewer processed potatoes and more food that looks like its source? Informally, many kids at my school don't know that fries are made out of potatoes. I believe it's a moral imperative that our students learn about real food now so that they can make better choices as adults. Feeding kids fries now will only encourage them to eat fries later. Fries are around three hundred calories of starch, fat, and salt that most people really don't need—and certainly not every day, which is how often some high school cafeterias serve them.

Admittedly, I see kids throw away much of the food that was formulated so carefully for their consumption. Nutrition directors considered children's preferences when they came up with menus for schools. The USDA guided them with their regulations. Although kids usually eat the school pizza, they also usually recognize bad food. You can't fool them with funny labels like "Salisbury" steak, chicken "tenders," and "cheese" lasagna (the "cheese" lasagna I ate crumbled like cottage cheese—nothing like real pasta). That doesn't mean that kids instinctively eat good food, but many kids know that school food is somehow different. They throw away the veggies, they throw away the main entrée, and they throw away the fruit, drinking only the chocolate milk.

At first I thought the pizza tasted like cardboard. Ironically, after a few weeks I started not minding eating school pizza. When I thought the pizza tasted okay, I realized my taste buds had turned against me. Experts say that people can learn to like something after repeated exposure over time. My sense of taste was devolving.

HOW DID I DISCOVER that at least some of my students could enjoy and recognize good food? One day I made a salad with a small group of students with autism. The occupational therapist and I had noticed that some of our students with autism lacked some basic self-care skills when it came to feeding themselves at a table, using utensils and napkins, pouring a drink, and passing a dish. I love being a special educator who can help children learn functional language while they learn valuable basic life skills that aren't usually part of the regular education curriculum (though maybe more basic life skills like nutrition education should be included). The occupational therapist and I planned a lesson ahead of time and informed the classroom teacher, who embraced the idea. The morning of our lesson, the occupational therapist and I bought lettuce, shredded carrots, broccoli, tomatoes, and cucumbers for students to help me create a salad. I brought in a cutting board, tongs, and a small knife. Another teacher brought in napkins, plates, and plastic utensils.

In the cafeteria, there is much debate about whether knives should be used (for safety reasons, it is rare to find a knife in a school cafeteria, even one that uses non-plastic cutlery). Most people are in agreement that cafeterias should ditch the spork and reintroduce real silverware, but bringing back knives? Fewer people advocate for that. Granted, knives can be dangerous, but usually flat, dull knives for basic cutting don't pose a threat. But maybe knives aren't the enemy; the food is. Where are kids going to learn how to use a knife properly? I don't even know how to use a chef's knife properly. Occasionally at home I still forget the proper way to hand a knife to my husband and he scolds me. I wish I had learned more basic cooking skills from my mother or in school—it would have saved me years of kitchen bafflement.

The occupational therapist and I were quite intrepid: We wanted the kids with autism to try chopping some veggies with hand-over-hand assistance. They didn't even know how to pick up a basic knife: At first a girl tried to pick it up and clench it in her fist. Was it possible she had watched *Psycho* too many times? We used hand-over-hand assistance to get them to use the appropriate grasp when they started chopping. It wasn't a surprise that they didn't know how to hold a knife to chop veggies because I believe it's only natural that parents would have restricted their kids' access to knives at home. What was a surprise was how quickly they learned to chop with hand-over-hand assistance—and they enjoyed it, clamoring for more veggies to chop.

Everyone participated in the salad-making in some small way, and every kid tried at least some of the salad and the fixings. One student who declared that he didn't like any veggies ended up actually eating at least half of his salad. I was proud of these kids. It felt like their resistance to salad and vegetables was due to lack of exposure—or overexposure to limp, reheated school lunch veggies. I believe youth of all abilities can be engaged in food preparation and hands-on nutrition education. I think they will want to eat food they make themselves, and I believe it's appropriate to give them those skills at school.

Parents in households below the poverty line who are scrambling even more than the rest of us may not have the resources or time to teach their children about healthful food and nutrition. If it is not being taught at home and it's not being taught at school, how will kids learn how to cook and feed themselves? And with schools implicitly endorsing fast food by offering it for lunch, our nation is paving the way straight to the local fast food restaurant—which is conveniently located right by the school in many neighborhoods.

I mentioned before that many of my students' parents are employed in the fast food industry. It is easy for them to bring home leftovers, food order mistakes, and expired food products. Free food is a great perk for people working at a restaurant, and many families rely on their employers for food supplements to stretch their dollars. But when students are eating fast food for dinner and eating it at school, you know that something is wrong. I don't think pizza every week is necessarily a bad idea, but I'm thinking of pizza with just a few ingredients: a simple crust of whole wheat, water, yeast, and salt; tomato sauce, cheese, and tons of veggies and some sausage. Who knows how many fillers kids consume on a daily basis when they eat school lunch and then go home to a bonanza of similar fast food items.

Kids in the Kitchen, Chefs in the Classroom

What better way to learn about food than to cook it yourself? Nutrition should be something you learn hands-on from a young age. Teaching kids to cook is the latest way that people are circumventing the cafeteria by bringing awareness straight to the classroom.

First Lady Michelle Obama launched Chefs Move to Schools to get nutritional knowledge in front of kids in an edible and hands-on way. Across the country, chefs have heeded the call to action and established organizations have expanded their reach into schools. In Chicago, Common Threads is an organization bringing chefs and low-income kids together to learn about cooking and culture. Purple Asparagus, headed up by Melissa Graham, is another nonprofit organization that teaches children to cook, reaching them at community events and at school in the classroom or during after-school cooking classes. In Minneapolis, Catalyst promotes healthy eating among teenagers, teaching kids how to become advocates by raising awareness and even getting them into school cafeterias to help prepare food. In New Jersey, Veggiecation, a curriculum-based lunch program run by Lisa Suriano, teaches kids about the wonderful world of veggies by bringing hands-on demonstrations into their classrooms. In the San Francisco Bay Area, Michelle Stern is in charge of What's Cooking with Kids, a certified green cooking school for kids. Michelle also consults with school districts about new initiatives like salad bars.

Being a business owner or founding your own nonprofit is not a prerequisite for getting involved in your neighborhood school. Ed Bruske, a parent and blogger at The Slow Cook, teaches cooking classes to kids in Washington, D.C., and in Brooklyn so does fellow parent and blogger Kim Foster from The Yummy Mummy.

The USDA grain requirement frequently gets in the way of a healthful meal. Sometimes I saw school pizza or a cheese sandwich paired with pretzels, which are considered a grain. Because the school had to offer more than ten grain servings per week, pretzels were thrown in randomly to bump up the number of weekly grain servings. I don't know how a snack food like pretzels satisfies the grain requirement, and the increased salt isn't helping anyone. I ate rice for school lunch less than once a month, perhaps because it only counts as one of the required grains. Rice was either served with "chicken teriyaki," which was a chicken patty (mechanically separated chicken, of course) with fake grill marks, or it was served in the Tex-Mex dish with beef or turkey or something over the rice. These entrées would include a random starch or grain to meet the requirement. Bread or chips with rice? It seems screwy to me. So I ate "chicken teriyaki" with a slice of whole-wheat bread. That is not a normal pairing!

Full disclosure: I loved the Tex-Mex dish. It was taco meat with beans and a smattering of cheese shreds over rice in a small paper bowl and it came with a package of tortilla chips. I feel ambivalent about tortilla chips: They do provide a grain, but they are loaded with sodium. A few chips aren't bad, but at least in my family, we have a tendency to go overboard. Whole-wheat crackers would be a better choice than pretzels, which are truly empty calories covered in salt. In the spirit of this fast food approach to kids' lunches, many of the sides were covered with corporate logos.

By ignoring lunchtime as a legitimate learning opportunity, Americans are paying a cost. We don't know good food, we can't prepare meals ourselves, and our health is suffering.

Calories from Fat

Readers of the blog assume that the school lunches I ate were full of fat. Although there wasn't a limit on the number of calories a lunch could contain, I found out that school lunches cannot include more than 30 percent of an individual's daily calories from fat, and must have less than 10 percent from saturated fat. Also, USDA regulations stipulate that school lunches must provide one-third of the Recommended Dietary Allowances of protein, vitamin A, vitamin C, iron, calcium, and calories. I never thought the lunches I ate tasted as if they were loaded with fat, but I can attest that often they were processed, salty, and starchy.

CHAPTER 4

Food Is Personal

- - - - - - - - - -

What is patriotism but the love of the food one ate as a child?

—LIN YUTANG

When I was a little girl, my mom and I would sit down with the monthly menu provided by the school and we would choose which days I would eat "hot lunch" and which days she would pack my lunch. The days I always chose the hot lunch were when turkey, mashed potatoes, and gravy were served. The mashed potatoes were slapped down on the tray and then a depression was created in the middle with the metal ladle where the lunch lady splashed in gravy with chunks of something brown floating inside. It doesn't sound that appealing when I talk about it now, but back then, it was one of my favorites. I still love mashed potatoes, but I have always been the kind of person who eats anything. I am the opposite of picky; as a child, I loved broccoli and relished baked beans. Now, as an adult, when I catch a whiff of the fast-food odor emanating from the cafeteria, I'm pulled right back to being nine years old and waiting in line again, even if I wasn't buying that day.

I remember eating my own packed lunch more often than I ate school lunches, mostly because I don't think my mom wanted me to eat that stuff all the time. I always made sure to have milk money and I remember enjoying both plain and chocolate milk. My mom would pack a bologna or a peanut butter and jelly sandwich, but I preferred bologna. In my family, my mom was notorious for her jelly-soaked PB&Js. I didn't like the two-to-one jelly to peanut butter ratio that she enjoyed so much. Semi-soggy jelly bread didn't do it for me, but if my mom *had* to make a PB&J, I usually requested raspberry jam, which fought more valiantly than jelly did to hold its own against a thick slice of überhealthful sunflower seedy, whole-wheat bread. Everything was whole-wheat in my house. I have no memory of Wonder bread or soda pop from my childhood. In fact, my mom waited so long to introduce soda that when I tried it, I felt overwhelmed by the carbonation and thought to myself, *Who could possibly enjoy this stuff?* My mom liked to put dried fruit in my lunch, wrapped in neat, little squares of plastic wrap. The other kids would be so grossed out by the prunes, but I enjoyed them!

I remember my mother putting notes in my lunch bag. I cherished seeing her handwriting on small pieces of paper: "I love you. Mom." It helped me get through some hard days. My family moved around a lot and we lived in multiple states. My most vivid memories of school lunch revolve around trying to find a place to sit where people would talk to me. I remember carrying a tray through a large cafeteria, racked with anxiety about where I would sit and with whom. Scanning the room with my eyes, I never wanted to eat alone, but I often did. Being new and little was hard. The ritual of school lunch is a very formative experience for children, and I can't help but think of all of these memories whenever I see my students lining up at the cafeteria every day.

ANOTHER VERY STRONG FOOD MEMORY is from the time when I ended up working for my mother in her coffee shop. In the early 1990s, when I was still in high school, my mom opened The Coffee cArt, a coffee shop located in Rhinelander, Wisconsin, that featured local art for sale on the walls. I was earning $3.65 an hour as an employee there. Since my sister was better behind the counter than I was, that became her job, which suited her—she was young, cute, and a lot less timid than I was. On the other hand, I primarily spent my days in the back room, balancing the books. (This was before Quicken.) My mom kept large ledger books that she filled with handwritten records documenting each day's sales. It was my job to transfer the numbers from long paper rolls spit out by the cash register every night to their appropriate heading in the ledger (under "coffee," "bakery," "soup," etc.), and then make sure all of the columns added up. I spent many frustrating hours pulling out my hair because the books were frequently off by just a few cents, and they had to balance exactly, as my mom was counting every penny.

My mother was an ethical businesswoman who was sort of ahead of her time. She bought many things locally. For example, most of the coffee she served came from Victor Allen's, a Wisconsin coffee establishment about three hours away. Sticky buns were always purchased from various local bakeries. I ate so many of them while working there that I cannot even look at one now. In fact, after the novelty of getting leftover sticky buns every couple of nights wore out, I started feeding them to our dog, Nanny. Eventually, even Nanny's enthusiasm for sticky buns waned.

As teenagers do, I often slacked off while on the job, and there were frequent fights with my sister after which my mom would order us both to go home. On and off, just like my moods, I resented "the business" because it kept my mom away, but I knew that she loved it. Ultimately, though, The Coffee cArt did not generate enough money to make a living, so my mom was forced to sell the business. After the sale, the shop went under within a few months. My sister and I were quietly devastated by the loss of something that had been so essential to our lives in a way that we didn't understand at the time. I'll never forget what it felt like to leave the coffee shop for the last time; turning off the lights, I was overwhelmed by tears and emotion. The Coffee cArt was located in a gorgeous old space with a cute antique geometric tile floor. Ironically it is now a Subway restaurant, and the old floors have been shellacked over and replaced with standard–issue Subway tiles. Mrs. Q was not even on the horizon for me, but I trace my food awakening back to that coffee shop.

At home, my mom cooked out of *The Silver Palate Cookbook* whenever she got the chance. She enjoyed preparing food for her biggest customers—my sister and me—and in turn, we loved to eat her creations. We never went to places like McDonald's as kids, because my mom thought their food was unhealthful. Most of our meals were prepared at home. As for my dad, I never even knew he could cook until after my parents got divorced and he started cooking for himself. It was refreshing and sometimes humorous to see him cook simple meat-and-potato dinners; and of course my sister and I liked eating his food, too, just as much as my mother's cooking, but in a different way. What my dad put in front of us was practical, not fancy, and a deep reflection of his personal style. My mom's cooking was always more complex; his was simple. For my sister and me, both were satisfying and familiar.

Since my parents divorced just before I left for college, most of my childhood was spent eating my mother's cooking. My parents' income fluctuated greatly: Sometimes we had enough money to go shopping for velvet pantsuits at The Limited; other times, we didn't have enough money to eat anything more than mac and cheese from a box (my sister's favorite, despite my mother's loathing) or baked beans from a can (my favorite). My mom was a good home cook when money was plentiful. Some of my favorite dishes of hers were her many pasta creations, her semi-dry hamburgers, and especially her homemade soups and muffins. We snacked frequently on dried fruits (including prunes), as well as on crackers and cheese. I remember a perfect, simple lunch consisting of nothing more than brie, whole wheat-crackers, a small salad, and some fresh strawberries. But the meal was especially divine because of the conversation over lunch that ensued with my mom. For our family food was always personal.

Many of our strongest, most powerful memories center around food. Those memories are created and a food culture is established at home. In chatting with my students, I found that many of them rarely sit down for dinner as a family. It's typical for Mom or Dad to work late or for the whole family to be on the go at mealtime, which is a reality most American families, including mine, face on a daily basis. But what about their meals at school? I want the time spent in the cafeteria to add value to the students' day. I believe that the school shapes children's experiences by either exposing them to new foods or reinforcing what is learned at home. When I thought about the quality of food being offered to students at my school, I realized how much they were really being deprived of.

Banning Lunch

In April 2011, a school in Chicago made news for banning students from bringing lunches from home to school, forcing all their students to eat school lunch. Um, wow. This sounds bad. I'm trying to follow the principal's logic.

To go to the extreme of banning lunches from home, the lunches students were bringing to school must have been pretty bad. This book is about how unhealthful the lunches many schools (including mine!) serve are, but that doesn't mean I haven't seen some awful ones being brought in from home. I have seen "lunch" from home consisting of two doughnuts. One student was sent to school with a banana and a bottle of flavored water. A reader of my blog wrote in that a kid in her school showed up with a can of pop and a bag of Fritos.

On the other hand, perhaps the school banning lunches from home actually serves great lunches. As I've learned, some schools do. There are schools out there that offer great choices, like brown rice and bean burritos, BBQ tofu steaks, pico de gallo, and kale crisps. Mmmm.

In France, taking lunch provided by the school is mandatory. You have to meet with the principal to opt out of the school lunch program. So it's not an unprecedented thing to do.

But what does bother me and my readers (including my husband) about this action is that it disregards parents' basic right to pack a lunch for their children, even if what's in it is unhealthful. Parents have the right to pack whatever they want for their children every single day. Two doughnuts? Okay. Gourmet chicken salad? Okay. Whatever parents want to do, parents can do.

I didn't get indignant when I read about this. The fact is, I like it whenever school lunch makes it into the news. The good, the bad, and the ugly—it all needs to be out there and up for discussion, so we can think critically about the issue from all angles and take action. Let's channel that passion and harness it to change school lunch, so that being forced to eat it is not a punishment.

CHAPTER 5

Peeking Out from Behind
the Curtain

- - - - - - - - - -

Once a word has been allowed to escape, it cannot be recalled.

—HORACE

When I first started the blog, I identified the state I was writing from as Illinois, but as soon as the blog got some attention I changed the location to the more general category of "Midwest," kicking myself for at first being so specific. I wasn't very good at conducting covert activities, I guess. Fortunately, though, I'd never mentioned my school district by name.

In March, I decided I would finally get back to some of the people who had wanted to interview me when I'd first launched the blog. By that time, I had eaten a total of about thirty-five school lunches and felt that I was in a better position to speak with more authority about issues of school food reform. Additionally, I felt a little more comfortable being in the spotlight, as my blog had been read by thousands of people each day. (And although I was constantly looking over my shoulder, waiting for someone to discover my subterfuge, nothing had happened.) So now, I found the courage to step a bit farther into the limelight, because when I thought about it, the benefits for my students outweighed the potential personal risks of exposure. Four months before, I could never have pictured myself doing media interviews or even having the chance to share my opinions on any subject with the larger world. But now things were evolving: It was an exciting time, and I decided to stop resisting and just go with the flow.

Gradually, I started responding to the e-mails. One of them was from a writer for AOL Health who subsequently interviewed me by phone; the day the article appeared, twenty thousand people visited my Web site! On Wednesday, Yahoo! picked up the AOL Health article and placed it on their home page. I didn't know about it until I came home from work and immediately logged on to the computer to see the story. I jumped around the house screaming in simultaneous fear and joy. My little boy thought I had an "ouchie." My husband printed a copy of the home page to commemorate the occasion. After I finished dancing, I sat down and thought, *There is no way I will be able to finish this project!* I was going to be found out now. People were going to ask questions. I put my hands over my mouth and stared wide-eyed at the screen. What had I done?

Next, I was contacted by ABC's *Good Morning America* for an interview. At first I thought, *No way; can't do it.* Even if I could gather the courage, I wanted to preserve my anonymity. I discussed it with my husband and my mother, who advised, "Duh, you don't turn down *GMA*." Okay, fine, I'd do it, but I just needed to make sure that my identity, or lack thereof, was preserved.

The people from *GMA* suggested shooting me in shadow and changing my voice by processing the audio with a machine that made me sound like I'd had a sex change and was now a large man of Italian descent. All right, that would do the trick. The day the interview was taped, I worked a full, normal day, eating school lunch as usual, and then I drove downtown to a swanky hotel. Here I was, a Chicago Public Schools employee who worked at a desperately underfunded school being whisked off for a few hours to a world of hotel fountains, high heels, and private suites to talk about school lunch. I couldn't help feeling like an interloper, but at the same time I was enjoying both the excitement and the further chance to spread the word, and perhaps help foster change.

A hotel employee directed me to an impressively chic elevator and I proceeded up to a very high floor. I was greeted at the door by a cameraman and a producer, who were welcoming and friendly. Anchor Juju Chang came around the corner and we chatted about family stuff. The producers and camera guys already had the lighting, chairs, and mics set up, so the interview got under way quickly. Juju interviewed me for at least forty-five minutes, though at the end, only five minutes of footage aired, including some shots of me walking along the sidewalk with her and typing on my computer (in shadow).

The previous week, Jamie Oliver's publicist had e-mailed me to let me know that Jamie wanted to speak with me when he came to the United States the following week. Would I mind sending over my phone number and some possible best times to call? I admit to being a little star struck. I e-mailed the publicist back with a list of available times. The day after my interview with *Good Morning America* was taped and the day before it was to air, I left work to go to day care to pick up my son. As I stepped out of my car, I looked at my phone and thought, *I'll take it with me just in case I get an important call.* I have too often been a victim of Murphy's Law and I was determined not to screw up The Phone Call from Jamie Oliver.

I went into my son's day care and chatted with Charlie's caregivers about my son's day. I got him bundled up (it was March after all) and we made our way to the front door. My cell phone rang just then, so I dipped my hand into my pocket to answer it, but by the time I picked up, the person at the other end had hung up. Looking closely I saw an odd number. It looked like an overseas caller. OH MY GOD, I'd missed Jamie Oliver's call. But then the voice-mail indicator flashed.

I couldn't be bothered listening to the message. I redialed the number and Jamie's publicist immediately picked up and handed me right over to Jamie Oliver himself, but not before informing me that Jamie only had ten minutes to talk. Jamie couldn't have been friendlier or warmer. We chatted for close to twenty minutes about our shared passion: good school food for little people. He asked me questions about my school and I answered as best I could. We laughed about some of the things I had seen, which he too had experienced in many school kitchens, in the course of working on his TV show about school lunch. We ended the conversation with us both saying in effect to each other "you are doing a great job," and he remarked, "If you ever come to London, I'll cook something for you." I hung up and immediately called my travel agent. (Yeah, I wish.)

The very next day, the *GMA* interview aired. It didn't come on until the second hour of the show, and by then I was on my way to work, so I didn't get to it until later, though my husband and my mom saw it live, which was thrill enough for me. I confided in a couple more friends and family members about the appearance and why I'd been interviewed, but I couldn't tell most of my family and friends. I didn't update my status on Facebook to announce, "I'm on *GMA*," even though that would have been fun. No, it was too important to the cause that I remain anonymous, even as I was trying to stage a revolt against school lunch.

And I did remain anonymous, though something was palpably changing. Thinking about the frenzy of media attention that my blog was getting, as well as the growing pool of eager guest bloggers I was putting to work, I realized there was a need for a gathering space, a forum on which people could come together to discuss food, health, school, and everything in between. As I looked around online, I noticed not only that there was no place for parents and others to chat about food issues as they specifically related to children and school, but also that there was no award or other public incentive for people who were working to change school food or doing anything meaningful in the arena of children's nutrition and health.

The weekends were a downtime from blogging about my lunches, so I started something called "Open threads," under which I would suggest a topic or pose a question as it related to a subject that had been mentioned on the blog earlier in the week. It soon became a popular way for devoted readers to speak their minds on various issues related to the blog, school food, or child nutrition.

I wanted to recognize people who were putting it all on the line for children's nutrition. After a discussion about sporks on the blog, ThinkGeek, the maker of titanium sporks, offered to send me a titanium spork, at no charge (they sell for about nine dollars each). When the package arrived, I opened it to find that ThinkGeek had sent me not one but five titanium sporks. My husband thought they were cool so he absconded with one, and I saved one for myself, which left me with three. I decided to use the three leftover sporks as awards I would give out, one for each of the remaining months of the school year: April, May, and June. Thus, the Titanium Spork Award was born.

While I had become aware of the main people involved in school lunch reform, I didn't want to be the sole arbiter of who deserved special recognition; I wanted the choice to be made by the community. So I wrote a blog post asking my readers to nominate people they felt should be singled out. They nominated people like Michelle Obama, Ann Cooper, Jamie Oliver, Kate Adamick, Ed Bruske, Dr. Susan Rubin, Chef Cipriano—all big names in the school food reform movement—as well as people I had never heard about. I created a reader poll on the blog, and soon it became obvious that Jamie Oliver was going to emerge the winner.

I still had Jamie's publicist's e-mail address, so I wrote to inform her that Jamie had won the first annual Titanium Spork Prize. After sending Jamie his spork, I had no real expectation of a response, which made it all the more surprising when, the following week, he gave an acceptance speech on his Web site's video newsletter (which was also e-mailed to his million or so followers, including me). Watching him say thank you to me for the spork was humbling and inspiring. Look at all he's done for the cause!

Winners of the
Titanium Spork Award

APRIL 2010—Jamie Oliver, *Food Revolution*

MAY 2010—Lisa Suriano, Veggiecation

JUNE 2010—Laura De Santis, Marblehead Community
      Charter Public School

SEPTEMBER 2010—Dr. Susan Rubin, Better School Food

OCTOBER/NOVEMBER 2010—Ed Bruske, The Slow Cook

DECEMBER 2010—Dana Woldow, Parents Educators
      & Advocates Connection for Healthy
      School Food

JANUARY/FEBRUARY 2011—Ann Cooper, Renegade
      Lunch Lady

CHAPTER 6

I'm a Pepperidge Farm Goldfish!

- - - - - - - - - -

The first wealth is health.
—RALPH WALDO EMERSON

One of the most frequently asked questions I get from my blog readers is, "How is your health? Has it been adversely affected by what you've been eating?" An important question, as thousands of children eat those same lunches every day. If my health was being jeopardized by school lunch, then what was happening to theirs? They were eating those school lunches year after year after year. Moreover, as Dr. Susan Rubin, from Better School Food, once put it in a comment on my blog, 180 days for twelve years is not moderation.

I am lucky enough to have very good health insurance, between my husband's policy and what the school system offers. Each year, we submit to blood testing and a "Health Quotient" survey, and if we are able to demonstrate that we are healthy, my husband and

I get a sizable discount on the cost of our health insurance, which is great. Sadly, that is not a privilege many of my students' families have.

Coincidentally, right before I launched the blog, I had a full battery of blood and other tests run, including levels of lipids, glucose, et cetera. Everything came back looking great, according to my doctor. It wasn't until I was a few months into the project that I realized this would provide a convenient baseline for any effects on my health from my school lunch project, and that I could actually find out if the lunches were having any impact.

After six months of eating school lunch, I revisited my doctor. By mid-June, I had reached the halfway point of my project: I had consumed 101 school lunches. Even though I knew it was for a good cause, thinking about having to come back in the fall and start back on the school lunch diet made me feel a little queasy. I still had those moments of, *Why did I decide to do this again?*—not least because my body was not very happy with me. I was hoping this doctor's visit would provide some answers.

I brought him up to speed on what I'd been doing. All that week I'd been wondering what his reaction would be. During that visit, I submitted to the exact same series of tests that had been conducted the previous December. The results were surprising: My cholesterol had actually gone down by twenty points! I chalked that up to how my relationship to the food I prepared at home had changed; I'd become hyperconscious of the food I was eating and of what I was serving to my family. Additionally, my blog served as an odd kind of personal food diary, and I'd observed that whenever people keep track of their diets, they tend to be more aware in general of what they are putting into their mouths. I was eating better at home than ever before.

My glucose level, the tests showed, had gone up, albeit very slightly—from eighty-two to eighty-seven, which is still within normal limits (over one hundred is cause for alarm).

Sound Bites from Lunch Ladies

A lunch lady told me, "I can't believe you aren't getting fat eating all of these lunches! I had to stop eating them because I gained too much weight."

The first question most people ask me is, "Did you gain weight?" Well, no. In January I weighed 152 pounds, and in December I weighed 149 pounds, which I consider to be a normal variance. Although I get the comparison often, eating school lunch every day was not the same as Morgan Spurlock's adventure eating McDonald's food for three meals a day in his film *Super Size Me*. His goal was to prove that McDonald's food was bad for you (and he sure did).

My goal was never to single out one school food corporation, one school district, one school. I didn't want to make myself obese. If I had wanted to do that, I could have easily "thrown" my experiment and gorged myself all day long. My modest goal was to raise awareness about school lunch by eating it. In the process of consuming the food, I was forced to examine how I was eating and my awareness about food increased tenfold.

Taking into consideration my height of 5'6" and my starting weight of 152 pounds, my BMI index was 24.5. The range considered "overweight" is 25 to 29.9. I guess I'm just mere pounds away from being considered "overweight," but no one I know would think of me as "fat" even though I have a post-baby "muffin top." Nevertheless, armed with my newfound knowledge about food and my family's increased interest in cooking from scratch, I have a feeling that I'll get into even better shape in the years to come.

It is not really my nature to talk about personal-health issues with people outside my family and close friends, but in a way my blog readers had become like my family, and (my parents would be horrified) I found myself opening up a bit, even discussing such intimate things as the fact that I had been diagnosed with Irritable Bowel Syndrome (IBS) in late 2007. I had gotten ill following a trip to China in 2002, and my digestive tract hasn't been the same since. At one point in 2007, I had taken a stab at going gluten-free in an attempt to determine if gluten was aggravating my system. The gluten-free diet did dramatically improve my symptoms, so much so that I wondered if I had Celiac disease, an autoimmune disorder triggered by the consumption of foods containing wheat and gluten. I went to a gastroenterologist and blood antibody testing revealed that I did not have Celiac disease. I was glad to hear that but also frustrated because I knew something was wrong with my body, and gluten still seemed like a logical suspect.

Later in 2010 at the BlogHer Food conference, I talked to food blogger Alison St. Sure, who has Celiac disease. I mentioned to her that I had been tested for Celiac disease a couple of times as I had suspected that wheat bothered me. She said, "You know, you don't need to have the diagnosis of Celiac disease to be sensitive to gluten." That statement ricocheted around my brain as we continued our discussion. That night I vowed to go gluten-free after my year of school lunches.

When I started the Fed Up project, I didn't think about my IBS at all. I just figured I'd be fine. I started drinking my pint of milk just like the kids, but I soon noticed that a couple hours after lunch I would have to make a run to the bathroom. I'm a slow learner: It took about two weeks for me to realize that I needed to cut milk from my midday meal. At home I switched to almond milk because I liked the taste. However, I did not stop eating all dairy products because I wasn't sure I would be able to do that—I really enjoy my cheese and yogurt.

There's Something in My Milk

The milk in my school's cafeteria is not labeled hormone-free, which makes me wonder—does it contain hormones? The hormone in question is recombinant bovine growth hormone (rBGH). It is genetically engineered and given to cows to increase milk production. The problem with increasing milk production is that it leads to infections like mastitis, which require antibiotics. I'm not opposed to giving antibiotics to sick animals, but what's driving the need for hormones? Does our country need more milk? The bottom line for me: I want my students to drink plain, pure milk with their lunch—no hormones need apply.

At the start of the school lunch project, I was also contending with the fact that my little boy, Charlie, was getting sick frequently. He was getting repeat ear infections, as often as every two weeks. In February, the ear, nose, and throat doctor recommended that my son get ear tubes. I was extremely worried when I learned that he would have to go through surgery, but after discussing it with some of the other parents at Charlie's day care center, I felt reassured. They told me that the surgery was a magic bullet: Charlie wouldn't have any more ear infections afterward, they said. *Okay, fine, we'll go through it and everything will get better,* I told myself.

Unfortunately within a month of the procedure, my son did get another ear infection, and the following two months he got two more. Still, I was grateful for what the ear tubes did: They reduced the frequency of his ear infections by half and brought advancements in Charlie's speech and language development, which I loved seeing. But why was he still suffering from ear problems?

When I was breastfeeding Charlie, I went completely dairy-free after noticing my son's apparent sensitivity to cow's milk. We were able to transition him to lactose-free milk, and his body seemed to tolerate that just fine. But now, as a little boy, he was regularly drinking cow's milk. As I researched possible reasons for Charlie's continued ear infections, I found a number of suggestions that removing milk from a child's diet was one way of avoiding repeat ear infections. Our doctor suggested just waiting it out until my son's immune system grew stronger and was better able to fight off the germs his body was encountering at day care. But I wasn't willing to settle for that, because I suspected the cause wasn't related to the colds but was more of a dietary issue, or maybe an allergy. To test my theory, I switched my son from cow's milk to vitamin D–fortified goat's milk, which is, by the way, about four times more expensive than cow's milk. (I shared this with a coworker who responded, "That's so very hippie of you!") I briefly considered soy milk, but I wanted him to continue to benefit from animal fats, since he was only eighteen months old. Happily, soon after making this change, his ear infections stopped.

But Charlie was still getting sick; over the summer we had to make two visits to the emergency room for breathing treatments. Our doctor was concerned about summer ER visits for two reasons: First, it is not the height of the cold and flu season and, second, in my husband's family there is a history of asthma. Also, around this time, after eating six months' worth of school lunches, I was diagnosed with mild asthma and given a rescue inhaler. Was this a coincidence? Could my asthma somehow be traced back to my new lunch menu? And if so, what about all the kids at school who were eating the same thing? For that matter, what about what my son was being fed at day care?

At Charlie's day care, meals are provided, which is convenient for working parents. Because it is a relatively pricey, high-quality child care center, I hadn't worried much about whether he was getting healthful food there—I just assumed he was. Occasionally I would pack him something special from home, but more typically, I just let him eat what the other kids were eating, aside from anything with too much lactose in it: no cream cheese or ice cream, but he could eat cheese or yogurt.

While I was in the process of making the connection between nutrition and health at school, I was realizing another relationship: the link between processed food and breathing problems. I read the menu of the food at day care and had a closer look at one of the boxes for "fish nuggets." I noticed that the day care purchased food from a discount grocer, which was to be expected considering the number of students they feed every day. By asking some questions, I found out that although sometimes Charlie and the other kids were served fresh fruit, more often it was fruit from a can. Even though the child care center employed a cook, the cook's job seemed to consist mainly of reheating things or opening cans, not preparing fresh, healthful meals. I hadn't realized it before, but I was discovering now that Charlie was eating processed food for lunch just like I was.

I made a change for Charlie. I took him off of processed food and cow's milk dairy products (he still enjoyed goat's milk). I began packing his lunch every day. After a few weeks, he did not need his nebulizer as often. He was still using his daily maintenance medication, but he was getting sick less often. He never has trouble breathing now unless he has a cold.

I was still eating school lunches every day and having the occasional need for an inhaler. I wanted so desperately to get off of the processed food, too, but I was committed to eating school lunch every day just like my students, who, unlike me, didn't have a choice.

This is one family's experience. Imagine the consequences of processed, unhealthful foods on an entire generation of children. The Centers for Disease Control estimate that more than thirty-three states have greater than 25 percent obesity in their populations and that one in seven preschoolers is obese. I consider obesity, malnutrition, and related health problems to be feathers from the same bird—something is wrong with our food system and our bodies are paying the price.[14]

Childhood Obesity Report: Solving the Problem of Childhood Obesity within a Generation

----

THE CHILDHOOD OBESITY REPORT WAS RELEASED by the White House in May 2010.[15] Its recommendations relied heavily on plain old common sense. The first set of recommendations relates specifically to the quality of school foods:

* *Update Federal nutritional standards for school meals and improve the nutritional quality of USDA commodities provided to schools.* My interpretation: They know Tater Tots should not be considered vegetables, but they don't know how to get that written into a law.

* *Increase resources for school meals.* My interpretation: They're broke.

* *USDA should continue its outreach and technical assistance to help provide training for school food service professionals.* My interpretation: They want to value "lunch ladies" as more than just servers, but as valuable school staff members. Can I get an "Amen?"

* *Schools should consider upgrading their cafeteria equipment to support the provision of healthier foods, for example, by swapping out deep fryers for salad bars.* My question: Is it supereasy to swap out a fryer for a salad bar? Is there some kind of exchange program?

* *USDA should work with all stakeholders to develop innovative ways to encourage students to make healthier choices.* My interpretation: They might be out of ideas.

* *USDA should work to connect school meal programs to local growers, and use farm-to-school programs, where possible, to incorporate more fresh, appealing food in school meals.* My interpretation: I love this but how do we accomplish it?

* *Schools should be encouraged to make improvements in their school meal programs through the HealthierUS Schools Challenge in advance of updated federal standards.* My interpretation: They want us to make these improvements on our own, without extra funds and prior to revising any federal standards.

The recommendations continue as related to other foods in school, the so-called competitive foods:

* *Increase the alignment of foods sold at school, including in the à la carte lines and vending machines, with the Dietary Guidelines.* My interpretation: If you're going to sell foods in the cafeteria, try not to sell crap.

* *Food companies should be encouraged to develop new products and reformulate existing products so they meet nutritional standards based on the Dietary Guidelines and appeal to children.* My interpretation: They want companies to make junk foods healthier.

I had to stop there because as much as I agreed with almost every word written in the Obesity Report, I found it tough to read. I saw a lot of support for the report online and what's not to like? Everything listed is wonderful. It's just that the goals are not written in a way that makes them measurable. Sure, the report says they want to bring obesity rates down to 5 percent (as opposed to the current 30 percent) by 2030. Fantastic! But what are our concrete steps? How are the goals going to translate into action? How are we going to overcome the major problems of lack of money, resources, and even time?

CHAPTER 7

Getting Chewed Up by
Corporate America

- - - - - - - - - -

It's hard for corporations to understand that creativity is not just
about succeeding. It's about experimenting and discovering.

—GORDON MACKENZIE

When I was an undergraduate at the University of Wisconsin–
Madison, I wanted to be a chemist because I loved science.
I successfully completed an enjoyable year of chemistry and thought
about continuing on to earn a BS degree with chemistry as my major.
After reflecting on it more deeply, though, I decided that working
full-time in a laboratory would not make me happy; chemicals were
interesting, but spending day after day with them was not what I
was meant to do with my life. I graduated in 1999 with a Spanish
major and a certificate in business. At that time jobs were plentiful,
and although I briefly toyed with the idea of working for a start-up,
I accepted a job offer from Kraft Foods in Illinois, trading in my dream
of becoming a chemist to take a position with a major food company.
I had no idea that, ultimately, a cubicle would be as dissatisfying as
a laboratory.

Working for Kraft Foods was a whole new kind of education. I was on the inside of a massive food corporation whose ultimate customers are families and children. I was only twenty-one when I started working there as a deductions specialist: Looking back I can't believe how young and impressionable I was. I was making more money than my own mother had ever made and more than I knew what to do with. I came to the position feeling idealistic and happy, and left four years later feeling exhausted and small. Although I already knew after the first three months on the job that it was never going to be the right fit for me, I stayed on because I thought that it was prestigious to work for a global corporation, and I wanted to follow my father's advice by staying in a "good" job, no matter whether it really made me happy.

As a deductions specialist, I worked with local supermarkets and other retailers and wholesalers to facilitate their payments to Kraft. I processed millions of dollars on my desk because the average truck carrying Oscar Mayer wieners, Capri Sun juice pouches, and Miracle Whip cost anywhere from $40,000 to $100,000, depending on the product mix. When I was working there, Kraft was making so much money that if a vendor shorted Kraft on a payment by $100 or less, they would not actively pursue that debt. It was considered below the "cash tolerance" limit. This was a far cry from Mom sweating every cent as the owner of a small coffee shop. I don't know about you, but to my family a hundred bucks is nothing to snort at; it's a week's groceries. The way I saw it, Kraft was taking a pocket full of change and dumping it into the garbage.

I found I just couldn't let that stand, so in my first year on the job I collected more than $1.5 million from vendors who underpaid invoices. How did I do it? I simply worked the phones, employing sincerity in my voice and personality to get the offending grocery stores to pay their bills in full. I was genuine in my indignation about these underpayments, but even so sometimes it all felt sort of pointless. In any case, Kraft Foods did recognize my efforts by promoting me, moving me to a supply chain position where I worked directly with buyers to fill customers' orders. If I'd thought that working in corporate collections sucked, supply chain and logistics turned out to be worse. I was happy when I shipped out trucks on time, but I only received calls when there was a problem with a semitruck in the middle of nowhere, or when a big Cheez Whiz promotion was not going to have enough product to meet demand. I didn't care about Cheez Whiz or the promotion, but I had to pretend I did. I got good at faking it.

Buyers would scream at me on the phone. "Where is my center-cut bacon? We have a promotion starting on Monday and that SKU didn't arrive on the truck. I need it *now*!" (A SKU is a "stock keeping unit" or code that distinguishes it from other products.) When there was a sale on hot dogs, a grocer would want to sell the whole line. If, for example, bun-length hot dogs didn't arrive in a shipment, this would make a vendor very unhappy.

I spent all day, every day, wearing a phone headset. Some days were so busy that I didn't have a chance to get up from my chair to go to the restroom. For this reason, even now, years later, I still have a hard time being on the phone for long periods of time. I have been conditioned to hate the phone.

One thing I learned at my desk at Kraft is that food consumption is generally flat. Plotted on a graph with time in days on the X-axis and food on the Y-axis, it is a flat line. Basically, you are not normally going to eat more tomorrow than you ate today. Yet Kraft would need to make a growth number for Wall Street in order to maintain its stock price. How do you make a growth number in an industry based on food if consumption is flat? Kraft Foods would oversell product to make the numbers. In some cases Kraft would *pay* vendors to buy more product than they needed at the end of every quarter. Additionally, food companies would go head-to-head to compete for consumer sales, also known as "share of stomach," which refers to how much a person will eat in one day. Kraft Foods wanted to meet their sales requirements and didn't seem to care that ordering should reflect true product demand.

Eventually I had an epiphany: I was never going to make a difference in the world sitting in a cubicle taking angry calls from disappointed buyers. As much as I loved my coworkers, after four years at the company, I left Kraft to do something else with my life that might help others in positive, meaningful ways.

Years later, when I launched the blog, I reflected on how corporations have to pursue profits so relentlessly, even to the point— at least in terms of the food business—that you have to wonder if they actually want people to overeat, to get fat, so that the flat rate of food consumption will start to tick up. When considering school lunch, the hand of corporations is also discernible. For schools where more than 60 percent of students live below the poverty line and will receive free or reduced school lunch, the federal reimbursement rate is $2.74 per lunch.[16] Initially it surprised me to learn that big corporations are even interested in small potatoes like that, until I thought about the sheer volume involved. In my school alone, for example, more than one thousand lunches a day are served. Multiply that by however many schools are in the school district and that starts to look like a pretty good business.

Reimbursement Rates

The reimbursement rates for free and reduced-price lunches from July 1, 2010, through June 30, 2011, for schools where fewer than 60 percent of students live below the poverty line were $2.72 per free lunch, $2.32 for reduced-price lunch, and when a student paid for lunch, the USDA reimbursed $0.26. Alaska and Hawaii received slightly higher reimbursement rates, as did schools with high percentages of low-income students (like my school).

And it is good business. I speculated about the relationship between schools and food companies after seeing that some of the food on my tray came directly from large food companies like Frito Lay. When I looked into it, I learned that school districts sign school food contracts with for-profit companies for millions of dollars. For example, Chicago Public Schools entered in a contract with Chartwells-Thompson to provide food service management for around $61 million for the 2010–2011 school year. That's school lunches, breakfasts, and some after-school meals in 450 schools.[17] Food Service Management Companies (FSMCs) then use commodity foods in addition to their own procurement to develop meal plans that fulfill the requirements of the USDA.

If I were a food company (like Q Foods for example), I would want to get involved in school lunch even if it was only break even. How fantastic to get Q Foods in front of tens of thousands of kids every month or so! Many of my students can't normally afford to buy brand-label chips or crackers; this only increases the appeal of these products. Actually I wouldn't be surprised if schools one day start selling ad space on lunch trays. I can imagine these food corporations eager to get their brands in front of a captive audience of children every single day.

I NEVER GOT TO SHARE MY EXPERIENCE WORKING at Kraft Foods with blog readers, but I wanted to, because I wanted to explain why I don't trust corporations. The occasional negative commenter would ask, "Who cares if kids are eating chicken nuggets and school pizza every week? Why does it matter if corporations supply school lunch? Kids should be grateful for whatever the school dishes up. If they don't like it, their parents should pack a lunch." It matters because there are millions of school kids who live in poverty and don't have access to fresh food. Many families rely on the school to provide a meal to their children so that the family can pay other bills. Even when families do pack lunches for their kids, many parents send their kids to school with cheap, "convenient" foods that are often highly processed and not very nutritious. It takes creativity and preparation to pack a lunch that is tasty, healthful, storable, and kid-approved.

What I did share with blog readers was my dislike of McDonald's. In July 2010, I posted a series of comments on this topic, which I didn't think would offend anyone, as it just seems obvious to me that fast food is crappy, and McDonald's is the most well-known purveyor of fast food. But when those posts went up, I immediately got a barrage of negative comments from people who thought I was judging them for liking McDonald's and accused me of being elitist.

It was then that I learned that even fast food is personal to many people, which was something I hadn't considered before. To them, it isn't necessarily about a corporation or whether or not a particular menu item is nutritious or healthful. It's what people are used to, what they know, what they have access to, and what they can afford. Indeed, fast food seems to have a strong hold on our nation's hearts and minds (not to mention our ever-expanding waistlines).

As with most of my investigation into school lunch, I wasn't sure of "the right answer"—so many things seemed murky. Many people want to get the corporations out of the schools, and, given my own personal experience, I am distrustful of the motives of for-profit corporations. On the other hand, I found out that some corporations are working hard to improve low-income students' access to fresh fruits and vegetables through local sourcing and farm-to-school programs. One thing was for sure: To get the corporations out of the cafeteria, there would have to be a huge groundswell of parents, teachers, and administrators pushing for change at the school level.

Competitive Foods

Many high schools and some middle schools sell food to students in the cafeteria that is not part of the official, federally reimbursable school lunch. The sales of "competitive foods" are used to supplement the funds received for school lunch, as many cafeterias are running at a loss. According to the Robert Wood Johnson Foundation, the top three competitive foods consist of chips, candy, and cookies.[18] High school kids spending pocket money on the occasional bag of chips or cookie is not a concern. I enjoy the occasional cookie myself. But with the widespread availability of convenient snacks and fast food around the corner from many schools, I think high schools should consider getting out of the business of convenience food. Moreover, when students forgo a regular school lunch for snack food, I worry that their nutritional needs are not being met. Let's empower students to make healthy choices through education so that when confronted with a decision over what to eat for lunch, they can make healthy choices independent of parents and teachers.

CHAPTER 8

Baby Carrots Can't Go
Outside to Play

After dinner sit a while, and after supper walk a mile.
—ENGLISH SAYING

At the end of each weekday, after most of the kids have headed home, teachers often remain at work, while the janitors start sweeping and cleaning. It's always seemed to me that those big open hallways just ache for activity, especially as the weather grows mild and summer approaches. Sometimes, the temptation of those expansive halls is just too much for me and I can't help skipping all the way down the corridor, in big, broad strides. But our kids don't have that option when school is in session. In fact, one day while I was retrieving something from the office, I heard a mom complaining to the assistant principal.

"Why do the kids burst out of school running at the end of the day? Every day my child almost gets pushed aside because all the kids want to get out so fast."

I wanted to jump in and explain, "Ma'am, your child and all the rest of the kids don't get recess. Not even five minutes to run and engage in free play. When you see those kids, so anxious, frantic even, to get outside, it's because their little bodies cannot stand one more minute pent up inside the school."

You read that right: At my school, there is no recess, which is increasingly true of many schools around the country. The only exception to this rule at my school is that preschoolers go out to play for twenty minutes, if the weather is nice. How pervasive is this trend? The journal *Pediatrics,* in a 2009 study, found that 30 percent of third graders, for example, have no recess at their schools.[19]

In the face of growing concerns over childhood obesity, it seems illogical to eliminate recess. But school districts are under pressure to fill students' short days with testing and academics and, taken at face value, recess looks like open space in the day. Practical considerations about staffing the supervision of recess and any liability concerns over playground accidents that might occur also have influenced those decisions. Additionally, with increased attention on schoolyard bullying, the elimination of recess curtails those opportunities. However, by cutting recess, many opportunities to increase positive social skills are missed.

According to the Clearinghouse on Early Education and Parenting, in 2001 nearly 40 percent of the nation's school districts considered modifying or deleting recess, and many new schools in Chicago, Atlanta, and New York are building new schools without playgrounds.[20] A school without a playground sends a message that play is not valuable, which runs counter to my training in graduate school, where I learned that most early learning happens through play. I have found that many social skills cannot be taught but instead are learned through interpersonal interaction. And even a school without a playground can still let kids run around on concrete. Recess can happen anywhere.

Through my blog, I've learned firsthand from parents, teachers, and administrators that even when recess is on the regular schedule, it is the first thing to get bumped in favor of things like tests and other school activities. So another message our students learn is that free, fun exercise apparently has no place at school. But the reality is that kids need spontaneous, free time that's apart from a more structured gym class. Many studies have shown that physical activity actually boosts classroom performance.[21]

Got Recess?

Most kids who get even a brief recess midday have it right after lunch. Little boys and girls rush through their lunches so that they can get outside as soon as possible to play. A *New York Times* article from January 2010 found that when kids have recess *before* lunch, less food goes to waste and students end up eating more of the healthful offerings on their lunch trays, such as fruit and veggies. Additionally, nurse visits dropped 40 percent. This makes total sense to me. Everyone knows that a surefire way to develop a tummy ache is to eat really fast and then run around!

For parents, first, verify whether your child's school has recess. If recess is offered, find out when it is scheduled. If it is scheduled for after lunch, talk to the PTA or the school wellness committee about the advantages of having recess before lunch. It seems like such a small change, but it could make a huge difference in the lives of your kids!

Are we going to treat our kids like little adults, or let our kids be kids? Kids need recess, and they also need more than twenty minutes for lunch if we want them to return to class refreshed and ready to learn. I heard from another teacher that there used to be recess at my school. My ears perked up. I asked around and found out that recess was eliminated about fifteen years ago when the school district "closed campus." I didn't know what that meant, but I kept asking the few teachers I knew who had been working at my school for more than twenty years. Students used to have a morning recess, a forty-five minute lunch period, and a short afternoon recess. When the school district found out that at some schools a few kids left school grounds and caused trouble, they "closed the campus," thereby abolishing recess. So administrators and teachers cut recess from the schedule for all schools, substituting a twenty-minute lunch period and shortening the school day. Now Chicago Public Schools has one of the shortest school days in the country, and the kids are kept inside all day long.

To help kids fill their stomachs in the short twenty minutes they are allotted to purchase and eat their lunches, schools serve foods that are supposed to be "kid-friendly"—foods that fill them up fast, such as Tater Tots. But in matters of food, as in all important matters, shouldn't schools be helping to *guide* children about healthy choices, not catering to assumptions about what children will or won't eat? One of the special things about childhood is that it's a period of life when we are constantly developing, learning at every moment. Lunchtime is at least as important as any other time in the school day. How much time do *you* need to eat lunch? Personally it takes me at least thirty minutes to eat at an unhurried pace.

I love food. When I used to pack lunch for myself before I started the Fed Up With Lunch project, I tried to eat at a more leisurely pace. I might get through my sandwich and an apple, then eat my yogurt at the end of the day as a snack. Other times instead of a sandwich, I would bring leftovers from dinner the night before, including pasta or rice-based dishes, which I carried in a small plastic container. In 2010, when I started buying school lunch, I rarely had the chance to finish what was on my tray, let alone to enjoy the rare examples of good, healthful food that were served every now and then. Twenty minutes to eat just wasn't enough time.

Let's take the example of a student I used to work with named Jennifer. She has short brown hair and bright brown eyes, and she lives with her parents and a sibling in an apartment not far from school. She loves listening to Justin Bieber and wears glasses, which really bothers her because she so wants to be "cool." Jennifer receives free lunch and eats the same lunches I used to eat during the course of the twenty-minute lunch period. Unfortunately, unlike mine, Jennifer's twenty minutes include lining-up time, which means that, depending on how fast (or not) the line is moving, she is left with a grand total of nine to thirteen minutes to eat, which obviously isn't enough.

Let's say Jennifer has only ten minutes left to eat lunch. This means she faces a choice: Since she can't eat everything on her tray in just ten minutes, what will she choose to eat? The nuggets and Tater Tots are quick and filling, so it's a no-brainer that she would select these, over, say, a bag of baby carrots or an apple. If there's a bag of chips on her tray, she might munch on these while chatting with friends. My point is, in the short times kids have to eat, they aren't going to have time to eat a balanced meal, even if that's what's being offered. I can't tell you how many times I've seen the students at my school drink their chocolate milk, gobble down a bag of chips or a cookie, and then throw out everything else on their trays. How can Jennifer or any other young kid be expected to be alert and ready to learn when their bodies aren't running on the proper fuel? And what does all of this teach kids about the value of eating healthful meals?

Schools are tasked with teaching subjects like reading, writing, mathematics, science, and history. You may think that just because it's not on the curriculum, students are not learning about nutrition at school, but you are mistaken. What's being served in the cafeteria does send a message about nutrition, just not the right one. Further, the lesson being offered via what's on those trays is not one that the Department of Education takes responsibility for. Rather, it's the USDA—the United States Department of Agriculture—that decides what goes on the menu.

Offering students a preponderance of processed foods, and little time in which to eat it, is a huge missed opportunity. My heart breaks every day when I think about how I've learned that other countries with equal or far fewer resources are able to provide their students with real food, cooked on-site. Guest bloggers from Japan, Korea, Croatia, and France have contributed lengthy posts with photos of the school lunches their students eat every day. The lunches contain fresh ingredients that are not processed—and the kids are eating foods from their respective food cultures: whitefish, sushi, and rice dumplings in Japan; seaweed and tofu soup with kimchi in Korea; barley soup and bacon pâté in Croatia; and salad, baguette with butter, cordon bleu, and crème caramel for dessert in France. It is evident that each of these countries has robust food cultures, which makes me wonder about my own food culture. Moreover, I have found out that in some countries, students even participate in the making of their school food. That is happening here and there in the United States, in some instances inspired by chef Alice Waters and her Edible Schoolyard program, but it is far from the norm.

Going back to my student, Jennifer, I didn't mention that she is obese. Her mother works at a big fast food-chain, so she eats a lot of fast food for breakfast and dinner. What she's getting at school isn't any better, which makes me worry that Jennifer's long-term health doesn't stand a chance. What lessons about nutrition and health is Jennifer learning from what's being served in the cafeteria? She's learning that fast food is endorsed by school, and that it doesn't matter how food tastes, since you can't taste food in a mere ten minutes. Finally, she is learning that scheduling time for a healthful lunch and for daily physical movement is not important to her school—so why should it be important to her?

At my school, like many schools, kids are expected to sit still and be quiet at lunch. And it's not the lunch ladies who are telling the kids to be quiet, but the teachers and administrators doing lunch duty. It's common to see teachers and administrators yelling at the kids to sit down and be quiet during lunchtime, which I understand, but still makes me wonder: If kids don't have recess, and they only get ten minutes to scarf down their lunches, when, exactly, are they supposed to get their wiggles out?

Since starting the Fed Up With Lunch project, I've become much more cognizant of the need for children to move. My training at Northwestern University taught me that speech is a fine-motor movement. Think about how fast your tongue and lips have to move and with what precision they need to execute the correct speech sounds. For most kids, it's necessary to wake up the motor system prior to sitting down and practicing fine-motor movements. I'll often start off a speech class by tossing a soft ball around, doing jumping jacks, or having kids form a circle, grabbing onto the edge of a small parachute and moving it up and down. Large-motor games are fantastic instructional tools via which to teach kids how to follow directions, and how to take turns. School administrators and teachers think a lot about reading and math scores, but maybe we don't think enough about things like visual/motor integration skills. I notice that when my students get warmed up, they are almost always more willing to participate in speech therapy activities; when they actively participate, it makes sense they will be more successful. I love seeing how well they focus after having a movement break.

In a 2005 study, *The Journal of School Health* noted that physical movement increases students' abilities to perform in the classroom.[22] It was during my training as a speech pathologist that I first learned this principle, but my later experience with students, not to mention common sense, reinforced the idea that increased blood flow to the brain helps a person focus and think more clearly.

Rather than complaining when we see kids letting off steam by running around and otherwise acting like kids, we should think about the fact that without a break during the day for physical activity, and without a nutritious lunch to power them for the rest of the school day, we can't expect them to perform and behave in a productive manner.

All kids, including my son, need time outside to run around and explore. At school, the only chance they have to do this is during gym class. Where I teach, this only happens once a week, which is just not enough to satisfy our kids' desires to move. One hour of gym just doesn't do it!

And if you won't take my word for it, what about the First Lady's?

Parents can use the Let's Move! Web site as a way to hold their school's feet to the fire. The site is filled with great information about the links between regular physical activity (including outdoor time) and the physical and mental health of kids. It is recommended that kids get a full sixty minutes of vigorous physical activity every single day, and via the HealthierUS School Challenge, schools that create healthier school environments, promoting better nutrition and increased levels of physical activity, are recognized for their efforts. Now that sounds like something parents can take up and help their local schools to achieve!

At my school, kids look forward to gym class. I'd love to see them get gym twice a week, but I think that would require an additional teaching position and that would be expensive. Adding recess back to the schedule makes sense to me because even though supervision would be necessary (which any school staff member would be qualified to do), I don't believe that schools would need to hire additional personnel. Since research points to kids needing recess before lunch instead of after, I want my students to get a daily recess starting mid-morning or immediately before lunch. A twenty- to thirty-minute unstructured recess would be ideal. In some cases, depending on the size of the school, two ten- or fifteen-minute recesses might better suit the students, with a morning recess of twenty minutes and an afternoon recess of ten minutes.

Getting Things Done

One mom and blogger in Texas took matters into her own hands. Corrie Meyer, who blogs at Just a Mom in Mesquite, approached her representative, Cindy Burkett, about the lack of recess in many schools in Texas. Rep. Burkett sponsored legislature (HB 3770) that would make a daily twenty-minute recess mandatory. Legislation takes time, but Corrie Meyer has proven she's more than "just a mom in mesquite."

Today's Free Play Is Brought to You By . . .

The vast majority of the students at my school don't get to go outside during the school day to play or just have some downtime. I really thought it was just my district, but blog readers have told me that many schools across the country do not have recess; and in the schools that have recess on the agenda, it is often bumped for school events including testing. There is only so much time in a school day, and it's hard to fit everything in, but I believe recess is critical to learning.

Thankfully my school does have a playground, which kids jump on before and after school, but I have read that many schools lack basic playground equipment such as jungle gyms and monkey bars. Every school should allow recess and have some kind of play equipment available to students. A couple of nonprofit organizations have popped onto the scene to help schools like mine learn how to do play right:

* Playworks is a national nonprofit that focuses on making recess a part of the school day again. They employ "recess coaches" to help teachers, staff, and students learn how to be physically active and how it can enhance the school's climate, making it easier for kids to learn. http://www.playworks.org

* KaBOOM! is dedicated to saving play for American schoolchildren. It is a national nonprofit whose mission is to create play spaces in schools and communities so that every child can live within walking distance of a peaceful place to play. http://kaboom.org

CHAPTER 9

Mrs. Q, Unmasked and in the Trenches

A hero is a man who does what he can.

—ROMAIN ROLLAND

My daily posts garnered many comments, and many of them struck home. Occasionally, people got excited and said, "You're a hero!" I felt sheepish when they went in that direction with their feedback. I am certainly no hero and, by the way, I definitely don't look like the storybook version of heroes, who generally wear flowing capes and look beautiful, without a hair out of place, even as they slink and crawl their way through elevator shafts or up the sides of buildings. I, on the other hand, still have post-baby weight to lose, don't wear makeup most days, and sometimes even forget to brush my hair in the morning. I am just a typical working mom who got an outrageous idea into her head and couldn't let it go. I guess I'm a little bit crazy, with a dash of determination.

One comment I received on the blog got me thinking: "Eating school lunch every day is one thing, but what are you *really* doing to help kids?" Ouch! That question really got to me. Even though I was joining the kids every day on the front lines of school lunch, that reader was right; there had to be more I could be doing to help kids eat more-nutritious lunches.

ONE OF THE THINGS I DID was help organize a wellness committee at my school. All school districts that accept reimbursement for participation in the National School Lunch Program are obligated to create local school wellness policies and committees in order "to set goals for nutrition education, physical activity, school food, and other school-based activities to support wellness." My school district had done its duty and established a wellness policy, but nobody seemed aware of its existence. Plus, there was no wellness committee to make sure a healthy wellness policy was being implemented.

As a matter of fact, the school barely even has a PTA. When I first started at the school, the PTA was hanging on by a thin thread; it was being run by teachers at the school—there were no parents in the group! There had once been an active PTA, but gradually parents had begun to drop out as the neighborhood changed and evolved. Finally after many years of encouraging parents to join with no success, the last two remaining teachers had almost decided to close up the PTA, which had pretty much become a TA. That would have been a new low for the school. Sadly, parent participation is practically nonexistent at my school for many reasons, but I am sure of one thing: For a school to effectively do its job, there has to be a partnership with parents.

I wanted to go to bat for our students and their families, so I decided to do something about the absence of a wellness committee. I teamed up with my friend and colleague, a special-education teacher named Mr. Marcella. Mr. Marcella brought in a third team member, a gym teacher who had expressed a particular interest in nutrition at school.

The three of us met together after school one afternoon to brainstorm. We decided to inform the principal of what we were doing before we got too far down the road, to be sure she was on board. Mr. Marcella emerged as de facto leader of the group. We liked his youthful exuberance and, perhaps most of all, his terrific computer skills. Our small team set about meeting every Tuesday after school for the next six weeks, working to refine a mission statement, to create a formal presentation for the principal, and to come up with a roster of proposed wellness-related school events.

One of our ideas was to set up a school wellness night in the fall. We knew that we could bring in the local alderman, a nutritionist, members of the local community center, and representatives from local "healthy" businesses to share ideas with the parents of our students. Our fledgling group wanted to create a school cheer with a short dance routine set to music as part of the daily morning activity. We wanted to get kids excited about school and give them a chance to have five or ten minutes of physical movement before sitting down to do their schoolwork, which we knew would help them stay focused. Since our students weren't getting a recess, and gym class was only on the schedule once a week, this seemed like a great way to meet the state's directive that students get fifteen minutes of exercise per day. We proposed limiting sugary snacks brought in by teachers or students for parties, offering such alternative ideas as making fun, healthful foods like salsa in class. Last, we drafted a letter to be sent home to parents, a list of suggestions for nutritious snacks appropriate for kids to bring to school.

After hearing our formal presentation, the principal expressed support and commended us on the creativity of our ideas. I felt tremendous relief to hear that she agreed with the basic tenets of our presentation, including our conclusion that exercise helps students learn. She confided afterward that she'd tried to reinstate recess at our school, but her attempts had failed. She didn't really explain why, but I reflected that recess might only get back on the schedule in the context of a district-wide effort, rather than as an initiative by one school. However, I did discover that teachers can request permission to hold what's called "teacher-guided" recess, an outside break based on a school lesson, which is something that the principal can then approve on a case-by-case basis. Getting daily recess back on the school schedule seemed like it might be tough to achieve, but I was heartened to hear that our principal had already been thinking about it and some of the other things we were contemplating.

Our spirits were buoyed by the reception our presentation had received, and we immediately started planning our next action items for spring and throughout the summer, so that we would be ready to launch in the fall of the following school year. Sadly, our great plans would not come to fruition that year. When Mr. Marcella and I arrived back at school in the fall, we learned that our third wellness team member had been let go. Our team was now down to two. And then we received a knockout punch. Over the summer, our school had failed to meet AYP (Adequate Yearly Progress), one of the requirements of No Child Left Behind. Our school was officially on probation! This was not good news for our school, and it certainly meant that our principal would have a lot of other things to think about besides our wellness committee. Wellness night was postponed indefinitely, though from our point of view, a focus on wellness was more urgent than ever.

Together with the student council, Mr. Marcella and I planned a green week at school for the following spring, including information about recycling and healthful food and coinciding with a field day to be held outdoors with competition and activities for the whole school to participate in. Nutrition and physical activity are vital parts of my students' education, and I still feel positively about the advocacy of our fledgling wellness committee. Organizing at the school level remains the most important thing that parents and teachers can do to change the school environment.

DETERMINED TO DO AS MUCH AS I COULD to be active in the school lunch reform movement, I also made it a point to spend my summer break—a ten-week stretch between school years and school lunches—doing something meaningful. Teachers view summer as sacred—in a way it's hard to understand if you're not a teacher (though students know what I mean). It's a time to travel or just stay at home with your own kids, for a change. I knew that I particularly needed a break that summer: not only a break from the food, but also time away from the computer, and instead with my son.

Now that I would be at home, I could make myself any delicious meal I wanted for lunch, but I couldn't help thinking about what my students would be eating. A parent of one of my students told me that she would continue bringing her kids to the school for lunch throughout the summer, so at least they could get a good daily meal. Summer Food Service Programs are operated at schools, churches, and community buildings to "help bridge the gap" for those children who are going hungry during the summer.[23] I was relieved that our school offers lunches over the summer, so she and other needy families can take part, and so that kids won't go hungry during those weeks. I wanted to think of something to do with my time and my blog that would be of added help.

I toyed around with several work or volunteer opportunities— including working as a lunch lady with the Summer Food Service Program in my area or even volunteering with Dr. Susan Rubin's summer camp in New York—before finding a good fit with Common Threads, an organization dedicated to teaching low-income kids how to cook wholesome and affordable meals. Their motto is "One Kid + One Kitchen = One World Discovered." While they have chefs on staff (and Art Smith, Oprah's personal chef, is one of the founders), they rely on volunteers to help teach the cooking classes and to assist the kids. When I contacted them, they assured me that the summer was a perfect time for volunteers to jump right in.

At Common Threads I wasn't Mrs. Q—just Sarah, a wife, mom, and speech pathologist, albeit with an outsized interest in school lunch. There was no need for anonymity here, which was a relief. Common Threads runs cooking classes year-round all over Chicago and throughout the United States, but in the summer they pare down their city-wide efforts and focus exclusively on offering a summer camp experience in the Englewood section of Chicago. Englewood is on the south side and suffers from many challenges, including having the highest crime rates in the country.

Common Threads has a well-established volunteer framework and can smoothly integrate new people. However, I found that after only a brief training, volunteers are pretty much thrown into the kitchen trenches, right along with the teaching chefs and the kids. It's sink (no pun intended) or swim. My own cooking skills

JANUARY 04, 2010

JANUARY 05, 2010

JANUARY 06, 2010

JANUARY 07, 2010

JANUARY 08, 2010

JANUARY 11, 2010

JANUARY 12, 2010

JANUARY 13, 2010

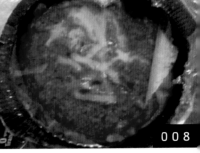

JANUARY 14, 2010

JANUARY 15, 2010

JANUARY 19, 2010

JANUARY 20, 2010

JANUARY 21, 2010

JANUARY 22, 2010

FEBRUARY 01, 2010

FEBRUARY 08, 2010

JANUARY 28, 2010

FEBRUARY 16, 2010

FEBRUARY 17, 2010

FEBRUARY 18, 2010

015

016

017

JANUARY 25, 2010

JANUARY 26, 2010

JANUARY 27, 2010

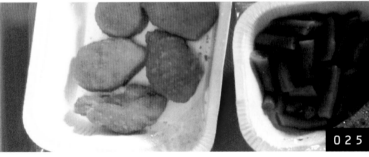

020

021

022

FEBRUARY 02, 2010

FEBRUARY 03, 2010

FEBRUARY 05, 2010

024

025

FEBRUARY 09, 2010

FEBRUARY 10, 2010

029

030

031

FEBRUARY 19, 2010

FEBRUARY 22, 2010

FEBRUARY 23, 2010

032

FEBRUARY 24, 2010

033

FEBRUARY 25, 2010

034

FEBRUARY 26, 2010

038

MARCH 05, 2010

039

MARCH 08, 2010

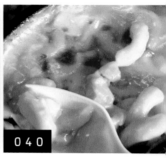

040

MARCH 10, 2010

043

MARCH 17, 2010

044

MARCH 18, 2010

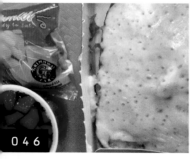

046

MARCH 22, 2010

047

MARCH 24, 2010

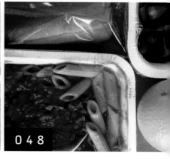

048

MARCH 25, 2010

035

036

037

MARCH 02, 2010

MARCH 03, 2010

MARCH 04, 2010

041

042

MARCH 12, 2010

045

MARCH 19, 2010

MARCH 15, 2010

049

050

051

MARCH 26, 2010

MARCH 29, 2010

MARCH 31, 2010

052

APRIL 01, 2010

053

APRIL 02, 2010

054

APRIL 06, 2010

058

APRIL 12, 2010

059

APRIL 13, 2010

063

APRIL 20, 2010

064

APRIL 21, 2010

065

APRIL 22, 2010

068

APRIL 27, 2010

069

APRIL 28, 2010

070

APRIL 29, 2010

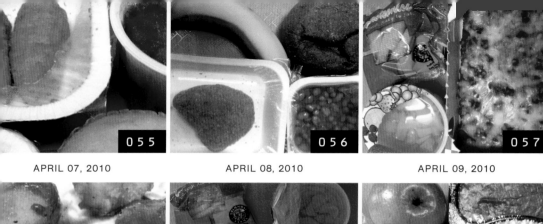

055

APRIL 07, 2010

056

APRIL 08, 2010

057

APRIL 09, 2010

060

APRIL 14, 2010

061

APRIL 15, 2010

062

APRIL 19, 2010

066

APRIL 23, 2010

067

APRIL 26, 2010

071

MAY 03, 2010

072

MAY 04, 2010

073

MAY 05, 2010

074

MAY 06, 2010

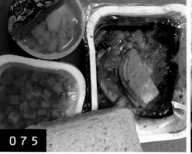

075

MAY 07, 2010

076

MAY 10, 2010

080

MAY 17, 2010

081

MAY 18, 2010

085

MAY 24, 2010

088

MAY 27, 2010

089

MAY 28, 2010

090

JUNE 01, 2010

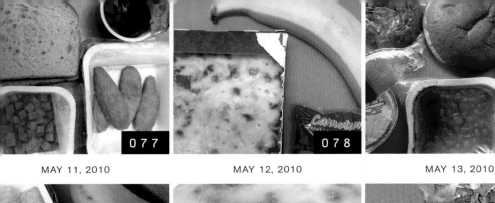

MAY 11, 2010

MAY 12, 2010

MAY 13, 2010

MAY 19, 2010

MAY 20, 2010

MAY 21, 2010

MAY 25, 2010

MAY 26, 2010

JUNE 02, 2010

JUNE 03, 2010

JUNE 04, 2010

094   JUNE 07, 2010

095   JUNE 08, 2010

096   JUNE 09, 2010

100   JUNE 15, 2010

101   JUNE 16, 2010

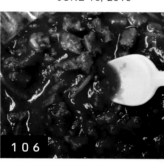

104   SEPTEMBER 09, 2010

105   SEPTEMBER 10, 2010

106   SEPTEMBER 15, 2010

108   SEPTEMBER 17, 2010

109   SEPTEMBER 20, 2010

110   SEPTEMBER 21, 2010

097

JUNE 10, 2010

098

JUNE 11, 2010

099

JUNE 14, 2010

102

SEPTEMBER 07, 2010

103

SEPTEMBER 08, 2010

107

SEPTEMBER 16, 2010

111

SEPTEMBER 22, 2010

112

SEPTEMBER 23, 2010

113

SEPTEMBER 27, 2010

114

SEPTEMBER 28, 2010

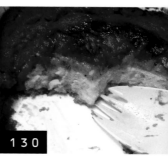

115

SEPTEMBER 29, 2010

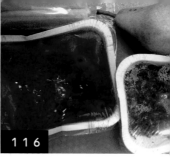

116

SEPTEMBER 30, 2010

120

OCTOBER 06, 2010

121

OCTOBER 07, 2010

125

OCTOBER 15, 2010

128

OCTOBER 20, 2010

129

OCTOBER 21, 2010

130

OCTOBER 25, 2010

OCTOBER 01, 2010

OCTOBER 04, 2010

OCTOBER 05, 2010

OCTOBER 12, 2010

OCTOBER 13, 2010

OCTOBER 14, 2010

OCTOBER 18, 2010

OCTOBER 19, 2010

OCTOBER 26, 2010

OCTOBER 27, 2010

OCTOBER 29, 2010

134

135

136

NOVEMBER 01, 2010

NOVEMBER 02, 2010

NOVEMBER 03, 2010

141

KETCHUP

140

NOVEMBER 10, 2010

144

NOVEMBER 09, 2010

NOVEMBER 18, 2010

146

147

148

NOVEMBER 22, 2010

NOVEMBER 23, 2010

NOVEMBER 24, 2010

137

NOVEMBER 04, 2010

138

NOVEMBER 05, 2010

139

NOVEMBER 8, 2010

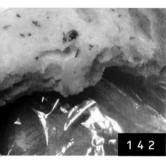

142

NOVEMBER 15, 2010

143

NOVEMBER 16, 2010

145

NOVEMBER 19, 2010

149

NOVEMBER 29, 2010

150

NOVEMBER 30, 2010

151

DECEMBER 01, 2010

152

DECEMBER 02, 2010

153

DECEMBER 06, 2010

154

DECEMBER 07, 2010

155

DECEMBER 08, 2010

156

DECEMBER 09, 2010

157

DECEMBER 10, 2010

158

DECEMBER 13, 2010

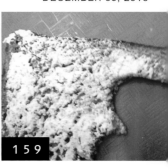

159

DECEMBER 14, 2010

160

DECEMBER 15, 2010

161

DECEMBER 16, 2010

162

DECEMBER 17, 2010

are pretty basic, and I have never taken a formal cooking class. Everything I do at home I either learned from my mother or got out of a cookbook. That summer, I learned at least as much as the Common Threads students did. Sure, I'd chopped veggies many times before, but I had never learned specific knife-handling techniques. I had previously cooked both rice and lentils, but never together in one pot. For me the experience was like taking a cooking class with fifteen other people, except my fellow classmates were eleven-year-olds. As enlightening as the instruction was for me, it was clearly thrilling for the kids. I witnessed their excitement at learning to cook and being taught how to prepare food themselves. The classes were filled with smiling faces and the sound of laughter, and, like me, they learned to use knives the right way—nobody lost a finger on my watch!

Aside from teaching kids basic cooking skills, Common Threads chooses recipes from around the world so that kids can learn about other cultures through food. Different weeks of summer camp were devoted to different regional areas, cultures, and cuisines. Cultural and geographical lessons were combined with whole-group and small-group instruction in the large professional kitchens in order to create a trio of dishes from different countries in a particular region. For example, one week the focus was Asia, and the kids prepared foods from the fare of Thailand, China, and India; then it was on to Latin America, to the dishes of Peru, Brazil, and Mexico.

THROUGHOUT THE SUMMER, I WENT HOME AFTER CLASS and came up with online content for the blog, but I noticed that I was also becoming a consumer of enlightening comments by others on my own blog, as well as religiously following others to stay on top of what people were saying about the food issues I had become passionate about. In addition to reading about the lack of ingredient transparency in school food menus, I started investigating how the food I ate made its way to my tray. Like so many things I learned, I can't say I necessarily enjoyed finding out what I did, but it was a necessary process, one I owed to myself, my family, my readers, and, of course, my school and students.

Michael Pollan, I'd discovered, is a revered writer on the subject of what we eat and what it means, as well as where that food comes from. Of course I was aware of him before my project, but since I'd launched, many readers had particularly urged me to read *Omnivore's Dilemma* to learn more about how the food system works. After reading the book, which I recommend to everyone, I decided that it was very likely that the beef I was consuming in the school cafeteria as many as three times per week had been raised on a controlled animal feeding operation (CAFO), or factory farm, and fed a diet of all corn (a way of producing beef that is cheap and readily available). At first, I thought, *So what? Who cares if the meat is coming from a factory farm and the cows are eating pure corn?* But then I found out why we should care. Cows are born with ruminant stomachs so that they can eat grass, but when they were switched to corn, they became prone to a host of illnesses, including increased *E. coli* bacteria growth.[24] I wondered why cows were eating corn. I mean, grass is free, right? Readers had mentioned "corn subsidies" in occasional comments, but I'd casually dismissed them as, well, esoteric. Corn subsidies couldn't be a factor in school lunch reform, could they? Again I turned to *Omnivore's Dilemma*, and I found out that our government subsidizes corn so heavily that corn costs farmers *less than* the cost of production. In other words, cows are fed corn because it is cheaper than plain old grass—it all boils down to profit over health. Just like learning about the USDA's oversight of school lunch, I was left scratching my head.

I REFLECTED BACK ON THE EARLIER, PERSONAL BLOG I'd maintained with my two readers (my mother and sister) prior to starting Fed Up With Lunch. It had no doubt helped me to understand the basics of blogging, but until I "went pro" I didn't understand how the reader connections one makes as a blogger can give you a platform, and therefore influence. Certainly, the fact that I now had an online presence was changing me, and I hoped my readers, for the better. I hoped that eventually it would have a positive impact on my students, too.

Another part of my online presence was my Twitter account; when I first acted on my idea to eat and blog my way through a year of school lunches, I also wanted to use Twitter as a way to share my experience with other people I might not otherwise have been able to reach. When I set up a Twitter account @fedupwithlunch for the blog and became an active user, Twitter became my PR department. I learned about Twitter "parties" (when an organization or a group of people sponsors a virtual chat about a topic) and collaborated with another blogger, Canada's @scatteredmom, to host a Twitter and blog party over one weekend in late August. We dubbed it a "Back to School Lunch Revolution" party. My cohost was even able to secure sponsorship from companies enabling us to offer prizes to our guests.

To participate in our Twitter and blog party, readers had to answer questions about school lunch designed to get them thinking and writing. Readers could link up a blog post with their answers, post a comment on my blog, or even submit a photo to answer the questions. Prizewinners would be chosen at random. We also sparked a real-time Twitter discussion of topics related to school lunch by posting a question every fifteen minutes, then awarded a prize to anyone who answered the question. I used the hashtags #schoollunch and #lunchrevolution because they were appropriate labels for our discussion. Some of the things we got readers thinking about: *Is school lunch an important part of your child's day? What is school lunch like at your child's school? Does school lunch need to be reformed? How much time should kids get to eat lunch? If you pack, what are some of the products you use to pack lunch? How do we engage more people in school lunch reform? How do we find out the ingredients in current meals? What nutritional ingredients are we lacking in overly processed school lunch? How do we start talking about "nutrition" instead of "obesity" in reference to school lunch?*

What came out of the blog and Twitter parties? I was able to reach more people outside of my usual circle of readers and raise their awareness about some of the thinking behind school lunch reform. Additionally, current followers of the blog were inspired to share their stories. I learned from a reader that in some school districts, chicken nuggets are served three times a week (in my school, we have a processed chicken product approximately once a week). Another reader shared that pizza was offered as an option every day at her child's school, and that they even had a limited "salad bar" where cold pizza was also available. She rightly observed that this meant a student at that school could eat pizza with a side of pizza every single day for lunch. Such information strengthened my own resolve: When I returned to school in the fall I would keep going.

While my summer of research, networking, and volunteering allowed me a refreshing break from my Fed Up With Lunch project, I was always conscious that I was going back to school in the fall to eat school lunch again and reassume my cloak of invisibility as Mrs. Q. After working with Common Threads, I more fully appreciated that kids need good food and that they love to be in the kitchen. I wanted my students to know the power of good food. I was hungry for success!

We can all be heroes in our own way by thinking about our unique gifts and perspectives and how we can use them to effect change in the lives of others. Look around in your community and seek out opportunities to volunteer at school or through a local organization. There are hundreds of little ways that you can make a difference.

Growing and Blooming: School Gardens

Many gardeners believe that the only way to change the food children eat is to have them grow it themselves. Alice Waters, with her Edible Schoolyard in Berkeley, California, has been a pioneer in the movement for school gardens. The Edible Schoolyard is relatively large and magnificent with paths, trees, and places to sit.

Admittedly, on the surface this model appears to be unattainable for an average elementary school. Schools are overcrowded both inside and out, and the idea of committing even an unused part of pavement to a garden seems daunting. I'm overwhelmed by the idea of the heavy machinery required to dig up pavement. But couldn't we just build a garden on top of pavement?

When I visited the Academy for Global Citizenship, I didn't see a "school garden" when I looked out at the schoolyard. During the winter, the garden was hiding in plain sight: Wooden boxes two to three feet tall and very long spanned the side of the children's playground. They looked like tall flower boxes, but in the summer they produced pounds and pounds of tomatoes and squash that staff members gave to students in small bags with recipe cards.

After talking to Los Angeles school garden–guru Mud Baron, I got the lowdown on school gardens. School gardens can be small and nontraditional, but their bounty can be just as transformative as large gardens. All that is needed to sustain them is the dedication and commitment of school staff members. And there is always plenty of help—kids don't have to be encouraged to get dirty!

CHAPTER 10

A Return to Routine Food

Don't judge each day by the harvest you reap
but by the seeds that you plant.
—ROBERT LOUIS STEVENSON

When I returned to school in the fall and headed to the cafeteria with my three bucks, I quickly noticed some minor changes on the menu. Maybe someone in food service management had read my blog!

First of all, the cafeteria had started offering salads served in little cups, which was an improvement on the container of over-cooked broccoli that frequently stood in for the vegetable serving. When I first saw salad being offered at the end of the lunch line, I smiled widely. I couldn't believe it. Granted, the salad was mostly light-colored iceberg (darker greens contain more nutrients), but I was grateful to see a change being made, albeit small, and I loved that the kids were getting raw veggies—the most direct way to benefit from vitamins and antioxidants. It can be hard for families to afford fresh vegetables when they seem expensive compared to purchasing "whole" meals from a fast-food dollar menu, which is why it's especially important to expose students like mine to fresh vegetables at school—they might not be getting that experience at home.

A Salad Bar in Every School

What do you think about salad bars? I never had one in school growing up, but my husband did in middle school. He said he loaded up on veggies all the time. I wish all kids could get the opportunity to serve themselves up a healthful salad every day with lunch—and thereby learn the value of fresh veggies.

Ann Cooper partnered with companies to raise funds for her Great American Salad Bar Project. I never thought about salad bars as being an American invention, but I know she's right about the need to get kids exposed to salad on a regular basis. And why can't we expose our nation's schoolchildren to this veggie ingenuity every day at school in the cafeteria?

The goal: Get six thousand salad bars into schools over three years. Your school can apply for a salad bar or you can make a donation toward a salad bar for a school. Visit Saladbars2schools.org to get more information.

There were other changes in the vegetable department—for example, instead of an individual paper container of frozen-then-reheated carrots, corn, or peas, occasionally there were individual plastic packages of raw broccoli. When I first picked up a plastic package of raw broccoli, I could have been knocked over with a feather. Was I seeing this for real or was it a mirage? Not only was it great for the kids to have access to a raw vegetable, but the packaging had been reduced from a paper and plastic combo to only plastic. It still wasn't going to win any awards for sustainability, but it was a step in the right direction that encouraged me.

Although there continued to be containers of reheated vegetables on the menu, these now contained a variety of vegetables, instead of just one kind. Mixing up different kinds of veggies in one package makes them more colorful and therefore more appealing to kids. I still saw a lot of the veggies in the cafeteria getting thrown away unopened, but my guess was that this had to do with the kids not having adequate time to eat, and not having high taste expectations of those processed veggies. I think that when menu changes are made, they need to be announced like a real event, and that taste tests among the kids should be offered at the same time. There probably isn't a budget for that kind of thing at most schools, but any kind of visual or verbal prompts by lunchroom staff members or teachers could serve to remind kids of the importance of trying the veggies.

That same fall brought much bigger changes at home when it came to eating. My husband, Mike, and I had been discussing food all year long. I shared things I was learning through my Fed Up With Lunch project and, gradually, it became one of our favorite topics. There was no need to sit around and talk about the blog when I first put it up, but after it gained some traction, it became apparent that I needed Mike for counsel, as my partner in crime. At first we talked mainly about the lunches themselves, but as I got more deeply into the issue, I started sharing with him things that interested me. We found that in talking about food in personal ways, and then defining it politically, it was not only my relationship to food that changed—his changed, too.

Mike had been supportive of changes I suggested we make to our son's diet as the year went on, because we were both upset about our son's tummy troubles and recurrent ear infections. We felt desperate for something to make Charlie feel better. When our son went dairy-free, and then a month later gluten-free, we noticed that he stopped having diarrhea and was rarely sick; it was hard to argue with those results. It was a relief to me that we both made the connection between food and health without having to disagree over these pretty radical changes to our lifestyle.

Mike had always been curious about the seeds from the fruits and vegetables that we ate, and he began to experiment, trying to grow jalapeños and avocados from the seeds of store-bought foods we consumed at home—he always got things to sprout, but not bear fruit. In 2010, he purchased an AeroGarden and grew herbs inside our house, sporadically throwing handfuls of homegrown basil into pasta sauces I made on the stove. Then, over the summer, he planted a garden and grew corn, jalapeños, and tomatoes; the corn turned out mottled and we had a good laugh about it, but the jalapeños and tomatoes were perfect.

That fall, Mike expressed a desire to learn how to cook, which was a very pleasant surprise. He knew how to boil water and fry eggs, but previously, whenever I had encouraged him to prepare something in the kitchen, he'd seemed intimidated or uninterested. Home chefs enjoy getting creative and even at times throwing caution to the wind. My husband was not the type to wing it, especially not when learning something new. Both of his parents are excellent cooks and they had taught him how to prepare one dish, cashew chicken, but he hadn't attempted it in many years. I didn't want to get my hopes up, as it was tantalizing to think that I might have some help in the kitchen. But Mike followed through on his plan.

He went to the library and picked up an Indian cookbook and told me, "I want to learn how to cook food that I love and I love Indian food." Mike took it upon himself to reorganize our cupboards, and carving out a couple of kitchen drawers for his own personal ingredients. He went out and bought a massive pan that barely fits on the stove, as well as a spice grinder. My husband was serious about his transformation into our new home chef. As his first meal he chose to braise a whole fish. We cooked side by side in the kitchen that night as our son darted in and out of the room, alternately playing with the dog and running over to give us spur-of-the-moment hugs. Being elbow to elbow with my husband in the kitchen was a new experience and one that I value deeply then and now. The first fish he braised was delectable and perfectly done, though it may have been beginner's luck, as the next two times he tried to repeat the recipe, the fish came out undercooked. Nonetheless, Mike was off and running. Food was becoming a central means of bonding and fun in our household, not just one more chore to do around the house; this is the way it should be.

Back at school, meals were more routine, and not nearly as much fun as they were at home. I mean, how much fun can you have in twenty minutes? Don't answer that.

ONE THING THAT WAS *NOT* AS ROUTINE was my growing confidence as a public figure. Still nervous about my secret identity, I was glad that I didn't eat school lunch at the same time every day. Sometimes my lunch break came at 11:15 A.M., and sometimes it came at 12:30 P.M. My schedule depended on when the kids needed me to be available. As a special educator, often I was in IEP meetings during lunchtime; on these days I asked a colleague who shared the speech room two days a week to buy lunch on my behalf. Although we shared a room, she had no idea she was purchasing a lunch that was going to be viewed online by thousands of people. Eating school lunch at different times each day helped me to stay under the radar. I didn't want the same teachers spotting me with a lunch tray on a daily basis, because more and more people were becoming aware of Fed Up With Lunch, and it seemed likely that at least one of my colleagues might put two and two together.

Occasionally, other teachers would buy school lunch, too. It wasn't a planned event, but now and then I would bump into them in the lunch line where we both handed over three dollars. Usually pizza or hot dogs were on the menu on the days when other teachers bought lunch. We would chat briefly as they walked back to their classrooms or to the teachers' lounge. Sometimes colleagues would comment on my food tray as I passed them in the hallway. Usually they peered at my full tray and then asked, "What are they serving today?" It was necessary to ask because the little lunch packages were covered in plastic and the steam inside them would condense, creating an opaque barrier that obscured the food. Other people would comment, "Meatball sub? Those are incredible!" Or "Hot dogs? I'll pass." One day when I was carrying a lunch tray with the Tex-Mex meal (still one of my favorites because it resembled real food), a colleague saw my lunch tray and decided she would rather make do with a granola bar. I somehow found myself defending the food. "Actually, it's quite good." I wondered if the school lunch masterminds had brainwashed me and changed my taste buds for good. The teachers all had their own unique opinions on the food, just like the variety of opinionated comments readers left on the blog. Like I said before, food is personal!

After many months of blogging, research, and media interviews, I felt brave enough to take on a terrifying challenge: I accepted an invitation to speak at the symposium held by the Mayo Clinic's Center for Innovation in Rochester, Minnesota. The conference's mission was to explore topics in health care, nutrition, science, research, and technology. The invitation came as a result of an interview I had done with an NPR affiliate about Fed Up With Lunch. A staff member from the Center for Innovation had heard the interview on the radio and decided I would make a great addition to their lineup—people thinking differently about health care and wellness.

I was flattered by the invitation, but terrified at the idea of speaking. But I finally said yes, as long as they could guarantee that my anonymity could somehow be maintained. I knew of the Mayo Clinic's reputation and how they helped patients like my grandmother and my aunt, who had made the pilgrimage to Rochester for extra-special care, advanced diagnostic tools, and world-renowned physicians. They assured me that my anonymous status would be honored. Like many things I have done while being Mrs. Q, I felt the fear but did it anyway.

Flying into the small Rochester airport, I asked myself whether I was doing the right thing by coming to the conference, though it was great to be back in a small Midwestern town again. But after getting to my hotel and meeting with a Mayo staff member named Richard, who was the head of IT and managed the Mayo Clinic's presence on Second Life (a virtual world in which Mayo kept an outpost and offered occasional talks on health care topics and research), I began to feel a little more comfortable. He was very warm and reassuring, especially on the topic of protecting the identity of Mrs. Q: We had previously decided that I would present my talk as an avatar on the Second Life, and now we talked about exactly how that would work.

At the symposium, I was humbled to be surrounded by some of the best and brightest thinkers in health care. I tried to figure out where I fit into this esteemed group. I told myself that the Mayo Clinic must have chosen me for a reason, and that I would find a way of living up to their expectations. Even though I was speaking at a premier event devoted to health care and wellness, being able to do so as an avatar was a great way for a normally shy person like me to ease into my role as a speaker. I was the only presenter who didn't speak on the stage. Instead, I spoke from the back room, speaking into a computer screen with a headset on. I had fifteen minutes to touch on the main points of my blog, and give the listeners something to take away from my speech. I'd worked on the speech for weeks and had it written out so I could read from it if I got too nervous. My talk received immediate, positive feedback. A number of people were surprised by things like how it is the USDA that controls school lunch, and the fact that my school, like many others, no longer offers kids recess. The people I spoke to in person afterward mentioned how "tragic" the issue of school lunch was. I had accomplished what I'd hoped to—I'd helped establish without a doubt that school lunch is an integral piece of the child nutrition, health, and wellness puzzle.

In October, I went to San Francisco to be a part of a panel at the BlogHer Food conference and speak about school lunches. After feeling that my appearance in Second Life at the Transform Symposium was successful, I thought going to BlogHer Food would be an even more logical fit since it was a conference focused on women food bloggers. Check!

When planning my wardrobe for the speaking engagements, I knew I would have to go out of my comfort zone, literally. I had to buy a new suit and new heels. It was my transformation into Mrs. Q, my anonymous alter ego. I walked from my hotel to the venue where the conference was held wearing a Tahari suit and high heels (instead of my usual work uniform of khakis and polo shirts, a holdover from working at Kraft Foods). But as I neared the door, I found I couldn't go any farther. I stopped and leaned against a short tree, planted in a square of dirt between the sidewalk and the road. I thought, *What am I doing here? What am I going to say? Should I have practiced? I'm going to freeze up. Oh my god, this is not worth it because my anonymity and the project are on the line. It's too risky.* So I turned around and walked away. Then I stopped again and told myself, *Stop avoiding this. Take a deep breath and just do it.* So I turned back around and marched toward the front door, my heart pounding. Anyone walking by probably wondered what was wrong with me!

I took a deep breath and entered the conference venue through a large glass door. As soon as I arrived, I felt enveloped in acceptance. I slowly and privately disclosed my online identity to people here and there, leading to deep discussions about food issues and family concerns. The networking during the conference turned out to be valuable for the cause of school lunch reform, and for me personally.

The BlogHer panel was structured with the audience in mind. I wasn't going it alone this time: I was part of a panel set up to discuss kids, cooking, and health under the banner "Our Food Future." The panel included Diana Johnson from the blog Dianasaur Dishes and Laura Sampson from the blog What's for Dinner, Mom?, with BlogHer's Elaine Wu moderating. When I first met Elaine, I chuckled to myself—we have the same last name and no one knew it because I was Mrs. Q. The moderator and the audience asked questions and we all jumped in to share our unique perspectives. The talk went well; I surprised myself by speaking with eloquence and passion. I found that my nervous energy dissipated as soon as I started speaking.

To say the conference exceeded my expectations doesn't really convey everything. It sounds cheesy to say it, but I was proud of myself for saying yes to unknown, hidden opportunities and taking a risk by attending the conference. I did get blisters on my feet from those heels, but I brought Band-Aids.

A Different Kind of Marketing

Cornell professor Brian Wansink made a startling discovery. By just changing a few variables in school cafeterias, he was able to increase sales of healthful foods. He used his experience in marketing to show that kids can and will eat more nutritious foods when the cafeteria is more appealing visually. Professor Wansink advised a group of schools to buy attractive bowls for the fruit and to use lighting to enhance the appearance of food. By incorporating attractive bowls purchased at a discount store on the lunch line, schools saw fruit sales double. One school used an extra desk lamp to cast a spotlight on the fruit. That school's fruit sales rose 186 percent.

Wansink also showed that adding a salad bar to a cafeteria increased vegetable sales, but when the salad bar was positioned perpendicular to the usual lunch line, its prominence increased veggie sales even more.

Professor Wansink even entered the debate about chocolate milk in school. He found that if chocolate milk was placed in the back of a cooler instead of out front, children would happily grab the white milk and not bother to reach the chocolate milk. Nothing like a little creative research to help fix school lunches.[25]

CHAPTER 11

Fruit Juice Is Pure Sugar
(and Other Things You Already Knew)

- - - - - - - - - -

Why does man kill? He kills for food. And not only food:
frequently there must be a beverage.

—WOODY ALLEN

I love fruit, and I've always liked fruit juice just as much as the next guy. I had never been a big fan of fruit cups, but after eating so many of them I actually started liking the taste of them! When I started eating school lunch every day, I noticed how many lunches contained fruit cups. After a few weeks of eating school lunches, I started bashing fruit cups on the blog. It seemed pretty straightforward that fresh fruit is preferable to plastic cups containing syrup and processed fruit. I had a policy of trying to eat a little of everything even when it all looked inedible. I made sure to be hungry at lunchtime by skipping any opportunities to cheat with a midmorning snack. Chowing down on those fruit cups did seem benign, at least when compared to the mystery meat rib-b-ques or bagel dogs, but still I worried about how much additional sugar those fruit cups contained.

And while I'm on the subject of rib-b-ques, the names of menu items at my school often made me scratch my head. Words seemed to be carefully chosen to gussy up processed food items that weren't so pretty in reality. For example, the rib-b-que sounded like a barbequed rib sandwich. But in reality, it was beef formed into the shape of boneless rib meat with fake grill marks somehow magically appearing on the patty in perfect parallel lines. It was invariably served with some kind of sauce vaguely reminiscent of actual barbeque sauce, but the sauce on the school lunch version was redder, more tomato-y, and tasted totally fake. I had no idea what I was eating.

Other fancy words on the menu included "pineapple tidbits" and "sliced peaches." Hey, those sound great to me! But often those appealing phrases actually referred to fruit cups that were in some stage of the thawing-out process. I know I ate frozen fruit cups at school when I was a kid. I remember getting them a few times and not being able to eat them. I remember occasionally even getting frozen milk. I hated how the shards of milk hit my lips when I put the paper spout of the pint of milk to my mouth. How disappointing it was, way back then, to be denied my thirty-five-cent milk during snack time!

But let's get back to the little fruit cup. Readers of the blog questioned me for belittling this popular menu item. I argued that kids should have fresh fruit at every school lunch. It makes sense to me that fruit cups might be necessary during the winter, but they also appeared during the spring and fall when, at least theoretically, there should be increased access to fresh fruit, including apples, bananas, oranges, and pears. Finally, a reader broke it to me: Fruit cups can sit for months, but fresh fruit has a tiny window of consumption because it has to be picked, shipped, and eaten in a short period of time. The hidden cost of freshness means that instead of fresh fruit, our children ingest high-fructose corn syrup (HFCS), as it is added to many varieties of fruit cups. As an additive, it does not offer much in the way of nutrition. In fact, a study out of Princeton published online in the journal *Pharmacology, Biochemistry and Behavior* in February 2010 found that rats given HFCS in addition to regular food gained more weight than rats given the standard diet plus water sweetened with plain table sugar.[26] And what's the second ingredient in chocolate milk? I'll give you a hint: It's not chocolate. Shhhhh.

Kids Say the Darndest Things

DAY
126

Taco meat with chips and a fruit cup was on the menu. The next day I was chatting with a teacher who told me my student had only consumed his chocolate milk and the juice from his fruit cup because he "didn't like" the rest of the food. I felt bad for this little boy because he missed out on a protein at lunchtime and I worried that he would "crash" later in the day. But I picked up a new habit from him. From then on, I started "drinking" fruit cups instead of just "eating" them because I wanted to try to do what the kids were doing—and I liked it! The juicy syrup didn't taste half bad.

Kids Say the Darndest Things | DAY 148

It was the day before Thanksgiving. Typically before a holiday, there is a sugar cookie offered to the kids. That day it was a maple leaf coated in red sugar. I'm sure it contained Red #40.

A student came up to me after lunch with bright pink lips. For a split second I thought, *Is that lipstick? Ooooohhhhh yeah, the cookie.* This particular kid's mom is anti-makeup for girls this age, and I wondered what the mom would think when she saw her daughter's lips. In fact, most of the kids came back from lunch with pink lips, pink tongues, and even pink teeth.

I asked a different student who had pink teeth, "Why do you have pink lips and teeth?"

"Because I ate cookies!"

"Wait, you had *more than one?*"

"I ate five cookies!!" He was smiling with glee. (Another kid piped up in the background, "I had two!")

"Wait, I thought you only got one? Did you buy more?"

It took me about five minutes to get the whole story. They did not buy more cookies. Some kids didn't want their cookies, so they gave theirs to other kids. The five-cookie kid was jumping all over the place and had a hard time focusing, constantly wanting to get out of his chair.

Another item on the menu that satisfied the USDA's requirement for fruit was the fruit icee. I call it a fruit "icee," but it is officially referred to as a "frozen juice bar." Actually, the kids call it "ice cream." I have no idea why they called it that, as the frozen bar is nothing like ice cream in texture, taste, or appearance. It is more like an apple juice popsicle containing food dyes and high-fructose corn syrup to make it look strawberry-flavored.

The problem with offering a "frozen fruit bar" to kids is that they get so excited when they see it, they eat it first. With a maximum of twenty minutes to eat, they almost always end up ignoring the more substantial foods on their trays. When they eat the bar first, they may only be left with a few seconds in which to chug down their milk. And that's the end of their lunch period.

School districts usually serve fruit juice to fill the daily requirement for fruit in school lunch. It's better if the juice is 100 percent juice, but if kids are only drinking chocolate milk and juice at lunch, they are assaulting their bodies with large quantities of sugar. Fruit is incredibly sugary, but that is fine when you it eat whole: The sugar is balanced out by insoluble and soluble fiber so there isn't the blood sugar spike that accompanies the consumption of fruit juice. I never thought of fruit as having fiber because it seemed like whole grains were the food items that had the most of what is traditionally viewed as "fiber." But fruit is really a perfect package on its own.

As a child I was a big milk drinker, though chocolate milk was not an everyday treat. My dad would mix it up using chocolate syrup at home. My dad's favorite was strawberry milk, which he also mixed up using strawberry syrup. I liked my dad's "homemade" chocolate milk the best.

Here you might be asking with an eye roll, "What's wrong with flavored milks?" Well, I might ask you back, "What's wrong with *white* milk anyway?" Milk is supposed to be white, right? The milk we drink every day should be the regular stuff with no added sugar. Sugary chocolate and its food-dye-containing cousin strawberry? They are for special occasions. Like birthday celebrations at home. Or in the middle of the night when you wake up to lights under your bedroom door, and stumble into the kitchen to find your dad mixing up a sugary treat. Times like that.

Chocolate milk contains three teaspoons of sugar that white milk doesn't have *and* chocolate milk contains high-fructose corn syrup.[27] Try teaching math to a room full of kids who just ate three teaspoons of sugar with lunch. Or try spending a few hours with them attempting to control their behavior. There's a reason I work with smaller groups of kids after lunch.

The dairy industry and people from the School Nutrition Association make comments about flavored milk, saying that if kids don't get their chocolate milk, they'll stop drinking milk altogether.[28] Really? Since when are adults afraid of what kids think? Aren't we supposed to be the ones telling them what they need to be doing for their health? I believe that it's okay if kids learn that chocolate milk is a treat, not an everyday staple. It's our job to provide them with the guidance and education about healthful foods, not cater to them.

IN ADDITION TO SUGAR, perhaps one of the most upsetting things about school lunches is the amount of packaging waste. One of my main gripes about fruit cups is that they come in plastic cups sealed with foil on top. It sounds innocent enough, but when many schools don't have comprehensive recycling programs for lunch and more than one thousand children eat one fruit cup per day, plastic fruit cups can stack up quickly in our landfills. When you think about how few of the children even eat the fruit inside, preferring to drain them of their juice, it turns into a larger issue of both packaging and food waste.

When I first saw the school lunches, I noticed that all the food was individually packaged in paper containers with plastic film on top. I couldn't believe it. I never ate fast food regularly so it was a shock for me to see so much nonrecyclable garbage being used. It just seems like too much paper and plastic! How did we get to the point where we think that tossing out tons of packaging eaten by tens of thousands of kids every day is okay? Most American kids know it's not okay to litter or throw garbage on the street, but then why is it okay to throw excessive amounts of paper, plastic, and food waste into our landfills directly from our school cafeterias?

In fact, the amount of waste in school cafeterias is tremendous! One thousand or more plastic sporks per day come individually packaged in lousy plastic wrap with a useless straw and a tiny napkin. That wrapping goes into the trash. The spork is ubiquitous in school cafeterias, but did you ever think that there's a generation of kids who aren't learning what a spoon or a fork is? I work with students who have special needs, who may not know or understand as much as some of their peers, but still, the number of kids in preschool, kindergarten, or first grade who can't name either "spoon" or "fork" is pretty staggering. On the other hand, they don't seem to know the word for "spork," either. It makes you wonder what exactly is going on—why is cutlery becoming like a relic from the past? Could it be because real food is becoming a relic from the past?

When you stop to think about it, you realize that many foods are now engineered to be eaten by hand. In theory, I don't see that as a bad thing because I love using my fingers to squeeze lime onto hot *al pastor* tacos and then hold the taco in my hands to eat. Food should be a sensory experience, and eating with your fingers can be very pleasurable. But I imagine that at my school, many of the foods eaten by the kids are devoid of attributes that would require descriptive words evoked by the senses. And, at home, kids are eating much of what they eat in school cafeterias: chicken nuggets, pizza, hamburgers, and hot dogs—none of which require the use of silverware. If you rarely use a spoon, fork, or, god forbid, a knife, how would you ever know its name? Sometimes, packaged sporks are even offered on days when the cafeteria is serving hand-held food. In those instances, those sporks are grabbed only to be tossed almost immediately into the garbage, unused.

When I began the Fed Up project, students went through the lunch line and each grabbed a large, plastic non-divided lunch tray. But when the teachers bought lunch, we were handed to-go Styrofoam trays. After I started eating school lunch every day, I rapidly accumulated telltale evidence of my new lunch habit in the form of a large stack of foam trays on a bookshelf next to my desk. While I ended up finding many recycled uses for them at home (under dripping plant stands and beneath my son's leaky vaporizer, for holding spray bottles and household cleaners), looking at the pile of trays I'd accumulated made me guilty. Midway through the fall of 2010, the Styrofoam trays given to the teachers disappeared and were replaced with paper trays similar to a paper burger basket. I was happy that the food service company was going eco-friendly. Still, this small improvement didn't change the fact that there are serious environmental issues that need to be taken into consideration in school lunch reform. My students were drinking the sugar juice from little plastic cups and then tossing the fruit and the plastic into the trash. It seemed unsustainable in the long run to devote resources to little plastic containers meant to be used once—not to mention wasting the actual fruit. I felt bad that more than 1,100 fruit cups would go straight into a landfill for just one day's lunch. When multipled over many schools in the district, the numbers started getting out of hand, and I wondered if our landfills could really hold all of it.

Would You Like Some
Red #40 with That?

When I saw bright red or green holiday cookies being given to students as part of their school lunch the day before a holiday, I used to think it was a nice way to celebrate. Now I wonder if those cookies were the reason my students would space out after lunch and have trouble concentrating on my lessons. And I'm not talking about the sugar.

Bright colors mean that food dyes are added to a product. Common food dyes include Red #40, Yellow #5 or #6, and Blue #1. Food dyes didn't bother me until I read that they are artificially created in a laboratory using petroleum as a base. I'm not really feeling the need to eat petroleum at lunch. If you are not as worried because you think a little here or there isn't a problem, start reading labels. Food dyes are being added to products that don't seem like they need them: cereals, snack foods including chips and dried fruit, even some oatmeal. I've even seen Red #40 added to packages of salmon to keep the fish looking pink!

All of the food dyes that I found in American products have been banned in Europe. European legislators are concerned about the link between food dyes and hyperactive behavior in children. However, here in the United States, we find them in many products including some of the foods I ate for school lunch. How much research has been done to make sure these additives are truly safe for kids to eat?

CHAPTER 12

The Bagel Dog Stops Here

One cannot think well, love well, sleep well, if one has not dined well.
—VIRGINIA WOOLF

When I was little, my parents held different viewpoints about food. My mom was the health-conscious eater and my dad was into junk food. He loved doughnuts, flavored milk, cakes, and cookies (bakeries in general). His first career was as a math and science teacher, but he left the teaching profession to earn his medical degree and has worked as an obstetrician-gynecologist for close to twenty years. Unfortunately, he is the kind of doctor who gives little thought to his own nutrition.

Eventually, my dad moved to California, so many of our important discussions happened over the telephone. Once I told him I was eating school lunch every day and blogging about it, months and months went by before he got around to reading Fed Up With Lunch for himself. After he did, he sent me an e-mail: "Very interesting.

To be the devil's advocate I think all the children from poverty . . . are lucky to be getting what they do! It is partially a matter of cost that they receive the prepackaged and frozen foods that they do. It would cost me and you and all taxpayers much more to supply fresh stuff year-round. The taxpayer is already supporting so many people in so many ways."

My response to my father is my response to anyone who doesn't realize what an important fight school lunch reform really is:

> *I just want you to know that's part of why I'm advocating for better school lunches. You know, we are already paying for these lunches that aren't doing much for the kids. There is so much waste in the system. Kids don't want to eat the food and throw much of it out. I believe if school lunches could be made better, it would end up costing around the same amount. What happened to lower-cost items like soup? Doesn't the packaging cost something, too? What about making fresh food on-site that all kids want to buy and eat? Teachers and students from greater means could purchase the lunches instead of packing lunches from home, thereby putting cash into the system. I personally would pay a substantial lunch fee to eat better food with my students and for your grandson to eat a good school lunch with his friends (when he gets older).*

> *If we think strictly about cost, we also have to factor in the costs of obesity, heart disease, diabetes, and other serious illnesses that students like mine have a good chance of developing later in life, since many of them have no good food model in their lives. If the school doesn't provide a fresh*

school lunch, nutrition education, or recess, my students learn that food is meaningless and that exercise has no place in school or a regular day.

If we fix school lunch, we might just fix our nation's schools. When Jamie Oliver changed to fresh food in the United Kingdom, science grades went up (8 percent), English grades went up (6 percent), and so did attendance (improved 15 percent).[29] At my school, reading scores are the ones that are the lowest (compared to math). How many schools would make AYP requirements if their students' scores went up by 6 to 8 percent? I would venture many, many schools.

So in sum, Dad, we need to toss out the processed food and bring in salad bars. It's an investment in children and their health. Extend the lunch period, throw in recess, a little nutrition education, and we'd be cooking with gas (pun intended)!

For somebody as stubborn as my dad, I knew it would take more than one e-mail exchange to change his mind. However, I knew I could quietly, slowly wear him down. I rarely stood up to him or voiced many controversial opinions because he was so outspoken that it didn't seem like a good idea. But this issue had taken over my life and my heart. I couldn't be silent any longer. Needless to say, he didn't send me another e-mail like that again. But he added in a subsequent e-mail: "PS. I can't see you getting fired. I would think you represent everything that is good about teachers and education . . . You will become a great positive example for the quality and caring of personnel at Chicago Public Schools." As one of my coworkers used to say, "From your lips, to God's ears."

Meatless Mondays in New York City

In New York City, the push is on to take meat off the menu on Mondays. Why? Because studies have linked the consumption of red meat with heart disease and cancer. Additionally, meat incurs higher transportation costs than plants do, which contribute to an increased carbon footprint.

When I read about Meatless Mondays, I was interested to learn more because I already saw meatless alternatives offered in place of the main entrée school lunch that I ate. Usually the alternative was a gooey cheese quesadilla or a cheese sandwich encased in crinkly plastic. I didn't necessarily see a benefit in going meatless those days. Plus a cheese-based alternative is still animal-based rather than plant-based, so it still contains calories with saturated fat.

Through Fed Up With Lunch, I found out about the efforts of NYC Green Schools (www.nycgreenschools.org), which is partnering with the national organization Meatless Monday (www.meatlessmonday.com) to advocate for going meatless on Monday in New York City schools. More than thirty New York City public schools are going meatless on Mondays. Reading the menu for some of their meatless offerings, I found out that meatless *can* mean flavor. Previous meals have included vegetarian chili with rice, black bean burritos, African gumbo, and veggie burgers with a side of beans. Dish me up, please!

"Accountability" is a buzzword I've heard frequently on TV. I define it as this: What happens in your life is your responsibility. Successes and failures are exclusively the result of your own actions taken in your life. The implied belief is that if someone is poor, he screwed up his own life. A lot of people who live in poverty rely on school lunch to feed their children. Yet it would be ridiculous to assume that families in this situation are somehow at fault, or—as my dad suggested in his e-mail—lucky to be getting any lunch at all.

The truth is there are often real causes for poverty that people have little control over. The economy has been terrible during the past couple of years. People have lost their jobs and their homes in large numbers starting with the 9/11 tragedy and then again in 2008 after the markets crashed and we entered a recession. I know what it's like to have a partner lose his job; we had to weather a period when my now-husband was unemployed for close to ten months. My point is that with so much out of our control, there should be no stigma around programs that provide free lunches for children who need them.

Some people argue that school lunch should be free to all. I certainly see why that is a compelling argument. The paperwork to determine if a student qualifies for free or reduced school lunch fees is thick and cumbersome; at my school, a secretary is taken off of her regular desk duties and spends the entire month of September working on lunch applications for the federal government. If all children received free lunches, this time-consuming process would be eliminated.

I believe that people who can afford to pack school lunch for their kids might actually pay for better school lunches. I would pay for better lunches for my child at day care. Better food at school would help me out. I wouldn't have to devote significant quantities of time to preparing and packing lunches. Additionally, my child could get a hot lunch instead of a cold one. Let's call it a "soup fee." I'd love to see my child get access to a daily hot soup with lunch. I'd feel even better if my payment helped out another student to eat a good meal along with my own son. Although I know that not everyone feels this way, it might work out well for my family.

Sound Bites from Lunch Ladies

I chatted with the lunch ladies almost every day. One told me about getting burned on the big ovens and warmers. They all have battle scars (anyone working in food service does). Then she said with a half-smile and a shrug, "[They] pay me to serve, not to cook." My heart broke when I heard that.

Now, while I'm on the subject of accountability, I want to bring up an important minority group that gets undue blame for everything that's wrong with school lunches. Yes, I'm talking about the lunch ladies.

Let's face it, the people with the most important jobs in relation to our health and well-being are the folks who feed us: our spouses and partners, friends, parents, and food service professionals, including lunch ladies. Lunch ladies don't have a lot of power, but they sure have an important job. They put food on the lunch trays of 31 million students each school lunch, every day.[30] How can feeding multiple meals (breakfast and lunch) to thousands of children each day be thought of so lightly? It's not their job to purchase school food from the suppliers, check nutritional content, or name the menu items. Yet most lunch ladies take the heat when there are food complaints, and those women are doing a tough food service job day in and day out.

I remember working in my dorm cafeteria in college and it was not easy. I was relegated to the basement to wash dishes. I will never forget the spray of the massive industrial dishwasher hitting my face as the trays came out or getting other people's leftover food sprayed on my clothes. After my shift was over I was always tired, hungry, wet, sweaty, hot, and covered in a smelly film of food grime. It was a requirement that I directly return to my dorm room and shower up or else I smelled like fried food for the rest of the day. It's no wonder some lunch ladies do not smile.

Lunch ladies are my heroes. I feel bad that lunch ladies aren't getting the props they deserve. At the school where I work, the lunch ladies are nice but strict. All of them wear aprons and hairnets and are constantly moving and counting the children. The lunchroom manager, Pearl, flits all over the cafeteria from behind the line to out in the cafeteria to chat with students and the occasional teacher. Usually, I see her as a burst of energy on the move, but she is still when she is talking to students.

Pearl is competent and well organized. To be that way she has to be exacting with regard to managing the flow of children through the cafeteria and the duties of her employees. Even though she is kind to people and I have rarely heard her raise her voice, I know that she is firm with her employees and tough on the kids when the time calls for it. Alternately, she is caring and builds relationships with the kids who need the extra attention. All kids should be so lucky.

It is not an easy job making sure that more than 1,300 kids get fed every single day. On top of this, breakfast is offered to kids who show up early and, when the after-school program is in session, she serves those same children dinner. Her efficiency would make a busy restaurant's kitchen hum. Conservatively, she serves more than two hundred thousand meals to the students at my school every school year. By that measure, the lunchroom staff are some of the most influential staff members in the school, as their work touches the lives of every single student in the school building and some staff members (cough, cough), too!

While I was doing the project and eating school lunch every day, I developed a relationship with most of the lunch ladies and the lunchroom manager. I learned about their families and their backgrounds. Pearl told me that she used to run a restaurant. I wanted to hear more about that experience, but there wasn't much time for chitchat in the few minutes it took for me to pick up my lunch. Plus, Pearl always had something going on, even if it was something as simple as searching for a lost lunch ticket. I wanted to ask her more questions about her feelings about the food she served.

Over the course of the project, I have been concerned about Pearl's reaction to my blogging about every school lunch that she served. I have seen how she used tough love with the kids. I mean, Pearl is your quintessential lunch lady: strict, even mean-looking at times, but with a heart of gold, willing to help out any student in need. I just hope that she will still be somewhat friendly to me after I reveal myself as Mrs. Q.

You know, I rarely saw Pearl take a day off. If I didn't see her when I was picking up my lunch, as I was walking away she would zoom past and wave. I guess I was one of her thousands of regulars. Lunch ladies build relationships with the students at school. Doesn't the person who feeds us create an inherent relationship? Building a connection with lunchroom staff, especially for the kids that lack stable homes, affects kids' education in a positive way. Pearl told me, "All of these kids . . . are my kids. If I'm having a bad day, I don't let them know so that they don't think it's them." I say we must start valuing the people who feed us and then we'll start valuing our food and ourselves.

WHEN I STARTED THE FED UP WITH LUNCH project, my awareness and comprehension of nutritional information was amateurish at best. Sure, I made an effort to offer balanced meals to my family by including a meat, a veggie, and a grain at every meal, and I bought organic products when I could. But part of why it was possible for me to eat school lunch every day for a year was that I didn't think food mattered as more than just basic fuel. I didn't think that eating school food would directly impact my health and wellness. I worry that so many of us are oblivious to the connection between food and the overall health of our bodies. I'm not sure how it happened but it seems like our collective knowledge about the simple power of real, fresh food has faded. The link between food and health is a dotted line. It's just easier to get something quick from a drive-through window or make something out of a box at home than to plan and cook a meal at home for the family. As a culture, getting back into the kitchen and eating at the table seem to be just as important as changing school lunch. In fact, I think the two ideas go hand in hand.

National School Lunch Week—Hug a Lunch Lady!

One week in October is devoted to the celebration of National School Lunch Week. Lunch ladies are caring people who work hard every day to feed hungry kids. I worry that lunch ladies are undervalued as staff members in the school.

We only spend one week a year celebrating the truly amazing school lunch program our country invests in to feed children at school. It's not a unique idea to provide lunch to students at school, as many other countries also offer school meals; but with the hunger present in our world, our country should be proud of this fantastic program and of all the people who work behind the scenes to make sure there is something on every hungry kid's lunch tray.

Take a moment to thank the lunch ladies personally this October so that they know you appreciate them. I'm definitely going to find Pearl and give her a squeeze!

CHAPTER 13

Put a Spork in Me; I'm Done!

I don't think much of a man who is not wiser today
than he was yesterday.

—ABRAHAM LINCOLN

I am not a fan of roller coasters. I'm terrified of heights and am claustrophobic. One summer when I was working at Kraft, they rented out the entire Six Flags Great America amusement park for an employee-only day. I was dating my husband then, and he was beside himself with excitement, just like a little kid. He went on every ride more than once: his dream day. I spent a lot of time waiting on benches, watching him shooting through the air, and thinking about life. I did get talked into going on two rides and while I was up very high on one—I'll admit it—I cried. It was all too much for me.

Eating school lunch every day and blogging sounds straight-forward enough, almost easy. But the food politics and the media exposure combined with the intrigue of my anonymity made the year a maelstrom of confusing emotions. Exhilaration alternated with jolts of fear. I relished the fact that when I Googled my real name, I got nothing. But when I Googled "Mrs. Q" or "fed up with lunch," I got thousands of links across the Web. Oh my.

Each step forward gave me an initial thrill, a paralyzing shock, or a moment of despair, but after the emotions wore off, I became more comfortable with my new reality, this unique identity. Sometimes it seemed like it was "just a blog," but other times it was my whole life. Being Mrs. Q for a year allowed me to become a school lunch advocate, my attempt at making a real difference in the fight to give children a better start in life. Whenever I had a crisis of confidence, I just had to look at my students' faces and remember their sweet spirits. They were why I ate school lunch for a year in the first place. They also helped me to find the courage to step from the shadows into the limelight.

A few months into my Fed Up With Lunch blog, I began to have nightmares about the project falling apart. There were days when I wasn't sure I could make it to the end of the year, and times when I was sure I was about to be exposed and fired from the job I loved so much. Not having control of what I ate every day for lunch was doing a number on me. I wondered out loud in a couple blog posts if I was developing some kind of weird psychological disorder that needed to be studied by researchers. I had fantasies about making lunch with my own two hands and devouring it. At other times during the school year, I started to love some of the food I got at school and wondered if it was some kind of food-based Stockholm syndrome.

Any of these scenarios could have prevented me from finishing out the full school year of eating daily lunches. But these dire outcomes didn't come to pass. Instead, I finally started to embrace the good energy my blog was helping to foster. I began to enjoy the ride and trusted that the good it was doing by raising awareness about school lunch across the country was not about to evaporate. I ate 95 percent (162 out of 170 total) of school lunches offered in 2010. And I reached a lot of people: My blog had more than one million page views by the end of the year.

I still shudder when I think to myself, *What if I had decided not to go forward with this idea?* I could so have easily dismissed it. I was *that close* to this whole thing never happening—and missing out on this great adventure.

So what kept me going? Whenever I felt unwell, afraid, or overwhelmed, I thought about how hard my students work to learn how to communicate. My students have communication disorders as a result of autism, hearing loss, or speech and language impairments, which can make it difficult to understand their speech. Even though communicating basic wants and needs takes time and they are sometimes unsuccessful in getting their message across to teachers and friends, they keep trying. They don't give up. Ultimately, I hung in there for my students. I was hungry for them to have good lives and to realize their full potentials.

Becoming a parent can be transformational. For me, having my son was like taking a wrecking ball to the old me. I came out of his newborn phase knowing one thing for sure: Charlie was it, the best thing I had ever done. From that moment on, I wasn't able to look at children as "other people's kids," as I had before. Now, every student I meet is someone's greatest accomplishment, potentially his or her life's work. What kind of education are these children getting? And what are they eating? Is their lack of good nutrition impacting their education?

Kids Say the Darndest Things

On today's menu was popcorn chicken. I asked a couple kids what they had for lunch.

"Chicken nuggets and milk!" and another agreed, "Yep!"

"Did you guys eat the veggies?"

Total silence. They were looking around the room.

"Did you eat the peas and carrots?"

"Mm, hmm," one boy responded, nodding.

I laughed. See what I mean about how they tell me what I want to hear?

Kids Say the Darndest Things

The dreaded peanut butter and jelly sandwiches! The next day, I chatted about the "sandwiches" with a couple kids. One boy told me that he loved the peanut butter and jelly sandwiches and that he ate both of them. A different kid told me that some of his friends did not want to eat the sandwiches and so they gave the sandwiches to him. I asked him how many he ended up eating and he said, "Six." Earlier in the project, I had snapped a picture of the ingredients. Each sandwich contains 318 total calories with 162 calories coming from fat, 33 grams of sugar, and 11 grams of protein. Doing the math on that, I figure my student ate approximately 1,908 calories with 972 calories coming from fat, 198 grams of sugar, and 66 grams of protein!

As I closed in on the end of my journey, I knew that I wanted to do even more to help the students in my school and kids everywhere. Eating school lunch every day was great, but what did it mean in a larger context? Sure, I'd changed my relationship to food from the ground up. And as my husband said one night as we enjoyed a delicious, healthful dinner, "If nothing else comes from this project, at least our family is eating better." But even though I was going to be able to stop eating school food every day, my students weren't. What could I do about it now that I was nearing the end of my year of school lunches?

I thought it best to approach it as a two-part action plan. There is first the "micro" environment—the school and its community. Then there is the "macro" environment, which includes the district and the country. My work on Fed Up With Lunch has been at the "macro" level. I never intended on becoming a major player in school lunch reform, but you know, there I was. The most logical place to start is at the "micro" level, where people have the most influence: in their communities. I had been working behind the scenes to create a school wellness committee with Mr. Marcella. I wanted to continue moving forward and hold a wellness night in the school.

To start changing school lunches, I needed to create awareness in the community about the need for change, just as I had done online.

There was still much to be done to raise awareness about school lunch within the community. In some parts of the country, wellness committees and fantastic school lunches are already a reality.[31] San Marcos Unified School District engaged its wellness policy with the larger community by sponsoring the first annual Wellness Walk in March 2011. The walk was held in the morning and was immediately followed by a wellness fair with games, entertainment, health screenings, and prizes. The San Francisco Unified School District has a comprehensive wellness policy that is available online and it goes hand in hand with their terrific school lunches. Two Chicago area charter schools, Academy for Global Citizenship and Namaste Charter School, have both received the USDA's Gold Award of Distinction in the HealthierUS School Challenge for their school lunch programs. Interestingly both schools work with two different food service management corporations to customize menu offerings.[32] Although the desire to change school lunches has been important to many school administrators and nutrition professionals, the money hasn't been there—now is the time to seek out creative ways to fund menu improvements.

Before I knew it, it was time to eat my last school lunch. I was emotional. It was a huge relief to be done, but I still wanted to contribute, just without consuming the food. I consulted with leaders and experts within the school food reform movement about their thoughts on school lunch reform and how to move forward as an advocate for changes in school lunch. Janet Poppendieck, author of *Free For All: Fixing School Food in America*, wants school lunch to be free for all students to reduce the stigma of eating a free or reduced hot lunch and to remove the paper bureaucracy that is created by lunch applications.[33] Dr. Susan Rubin, founder of Better School Food and one of the parents from the documentary *Two Angry Moms*, advocates for a school garden at every school.[34] Chef Ann Cooper, "renegade lunch lady" and founder of The Lunch Box, wants to put a salad bar in every school.[35] Jamie Oliver says that in addition to finding out what their children are eating at school, people need to more generally educate themselves about food and cooking.[36]

Wanting kids to succeed is universal. To bring about change, we need to mobilize all parents to take an active role in their children's education. Because of my experience in special education, I know that a child's parents can be a powerful force in shaping the education of their children. Reading a school lunch menu does not a lunch reform advocate make. It's time to get into the cafeteria and start asking respectful, thoughtful questions without turning people off. It's just a matter of getting people aware and engaged about food so that healthy eating can be reinforced both at school and at home to really make a difference. When parents and teachers combine forces, there is nothing that children cannot accomplish.

We think about reading and math (and in my case communication) as being the foundation of an education. Let's go back to one of our basic needs: food. We're testing, testing, and testing the quality of education as it relates to our students' abilities in reading and math, but no one has yet to put the food to the test. There are terrific pockets of change occurring across our country, but some school districts haven't thought about nutrition as the groundwork to academic performance. The food in the school environment has to be the best if we are serious about academic achievement for all. Lunchtime needs to be longer than twenty minutes. Kids need a minimum of thirty minutes to eat lunch. While we're at it, let's push for a salad bar in every school to increase students' access to fresh vegetables. I believe that integrating nutrition education with menu changes is vital so that students learn and understand the rationale for menu changes and the importance of eating healthfully. Make ingredient transparency a priority, as parents deserve the right to see exactly what their children are eating every day. Enough with the processed chicken—let's toss out the processed "kid-friendly" food and do a better job of keeping foods whole. To decrease the presence of processed meat products on the menu, let's incorporate Meatless Monday nationwide with creative meatless lunches that don't consist of gooey processed cheese. Let's move away from cupcakes as the default way to celebrate birthdays and holidays in the classroom and reserve chocolate milk as a treat for outside of school—not a daily expectation. Kids need movement breaks, so I advocate twenty to thirty minutes of unstructured recess every day. Let's start a wellness committee in every school made up of active and concerned parents and teachers—including an involved student or two. The time is now, as issues about nutrition and physical activity have never been more pressing for the health of our nation.

Being Mrs. Q taught me that anything is possible. I had heard it before, but I had never truly believed it. I used the meager tools of my stomach and my cell phone to turn into a poster child (poster woman!) for school lunch reform. It is testament to the power of technology and the power of one voice. I never imagined I'd get through all of those lunches! But one person can make change; one person can be the difference. Your voice matters. If we band together, teachers, parents, lunch ladies, and administrators, there is nothing we can't fix in our children's schools.

Mrs. Q's Guide to Quiet Revolution:
An Action and Resource Guide

Now that you are aware of some of the problems related to school lunch, what can you do? Are you like me, in that you probably wouldn't picket the offices of the school board or storm the USDA? If you want to march around with a sign, I say go for it—and now that I'm out, I might even join you. But the reality is that many people prefer to advocate for change in more subtle ways that are also meaningful and effective.

School lunch is such a big, complex problem that it's hard to imagine finding one way to tackle it. There is variability between states and regions of the country, urban and rural settings, as well as school districts and schools. Each one of us relates to our neighborhood school differently, as a parent, teacher, nutrition professional, chef, or concerned neighbor. Everyone can participate and do something to advocate for change— any action, no matter how big or small, is important. It's the act of doing something that matters.

The guide I have written in the following pages is based upon my experience working in an underfunded, urban setting for five years. I realize that other school systems have stronger parent-teacher associations (PTAs), more funding for school activities, and more parent advocacy in general. While my recommendations may not apply to all of you, I hope that what I share is a useful introduction on how to be an advocate. For those of you with more experience, I hope to inspire further ideas that you can apply in your own communities.

PARENTS

Parents have the best opportunity to become advocates for their children's schools. There is no substitute for being there. Every parent can request to have lunch with his or her child at school in the lunchroom. You might be the first person ever to ask to do this, or it could be routine to have a parent present at lunchtime.

But don't feel like you have to show up and eat school lunch with your child all by yourself. Casually ask your friends and fellow parents to join you. Use Facebook to announce, "I'm going to volunteer in Joe's class [or attend the book fair with Joe at school] today—who else is going and wants to stay for school lunch in the cafeteria?" Then you can report back to Facebook with the results of your expedition, or tweet your experience and observations on Twitter to share them with a wider audience, including me (@fedupwithlunch) and anyone who searches for "school lunch." Consider taking some discreet cell phone photos to document what you saw and sharing them on a Web site like Flickr with a tagline "school lunch." Anyone searching for photos of school lunch can find yours and comment. That's some powerful testimony!

Some questions to consider when dining with your child:

* How much time does your child have for lunch?

* Are the lunches cooked on-site or brought in by a company?

* Is there a choice among food items? What does your child prefer?

- How much does your child pay and does he/she pay by paper ticket or by entering a PIN on a keypad?

- Observe the lunch line, the kitchen, and the cafeteria. Is it noisy and chaotic? Is there enough space? Is there adequate lunchroom supervision?

- Are the children eating their food? Do they have trouble with the packaging?

- How much of their lunch can children eat in the time allowed? What are the students throwing away?

- Is there recess before lunch, after lunch, or not at all?

The answers to these questions will guide you. Some parents have mentioned being pleasantly surprised by the experience of eating with their children, while other parents have been shocked. I don't have a school-age child, but when I have observed my son's day care at lunch, it was then that I realized that all of the veggies and fruit were from cans. Reading the menu alone did not give me that information.

If you are in the PTA, now is the time to speak up about the issue of school lunch. Did you know that if your school takes federally subsidized lunches, the district is required to have a local school wellness policy? A school wellness policy is a plan of action written by parents and teachers describing the school environment as it pertains to nutrition and physical activity. The policy is written to guide decisions made by teachers and staff within the school district. And it encourages schools within a school district to create local wellness committees. The school wellness policy is not meant to be left on paper but to be implemented at the school level. If there isn't a school wellness committee at your school, you can start one.

One parent cannot do it alone—you will need to recruit. As I said before, you can use social networking sites to engage friends and fellow parents, or simply pick up the phone. Observe the parents who are at school a lot and approach them.

Think about your relationship with your child's teacher. Involving teachers is important because when you head into the principal's office to discuss these issues, you'll get more traction with a teacher by your side. Do you feel comfortable talking with that person and even exploring school issues with him or her? If you do, I would recommend a subtle, respectful approach to gauge the teacher's interest in school lunch reform. Good questions to start with:

* What do you think about our school's lunch program?

* Do you think there is room for improvement?

* Do you know who provides the meals and whether they are cooked on-site?

If your student's teacher is able to answer those questions and engages you in a discussion, explain to him or her the importance of making sure that all students in the school get the best nutrition possible so that they can perform their best at school. Some follow-up questions include:

* How do you manage classroom snacks and rewards?

* Is there an active PTA or school wellness committee and are you participating?

* Have you talked to the principal about your concerns?

* I am interested in learning more about starting up a school wellness committee—would you like to join me?

If your child's teacher does not seem interested, there are other staff members within the school building who might be amenable to discussing school lunch and reform.

Did you know that ancillary staff is required to be present for parent-teacher conferences? I'm a speech pathologist and I am required to be present in the building during parent-teacher conferences (which are called "report card pickup day" in Chicago Public Schools). While parents usually make a point of visiting their child's classroom teacher, some of my students' parents don't stop by to discuss their children's progress in speech. Granted, I do see parents at yearly individual education plan (IEP) meetings, but since I'm in the school building during conferences, parents might as well take advantage of my presence.

I think it's important to visit all the teachers and staff who interact with your child. I encourage all parents to do this. After you've chatted with your student's classroom teacher, the second school professional to approach is the physical education/gym teacher. During parent-teacher conferences, often physical education teachers are free to discuss parents' concerns about students' health and well-being because, just like me, they don't have a steady line of parents waiting to chat. Did you know that written into the state learning standards for physical education is instruction on the food pyramid? Physical education teachers are perfect to engage in a discussion because they have a real stake in child nutrition and wellness and, just like all public school teachers, they have to base their lesson plans on the state learning standards.

When you are visiting the school for parent-teacher conferences or school open houses, stop by the cafeteria. Observe the size of the space, the structure of the lunch lines, and the kitchen. Is there room to prepare food? If you are there during lunchtime, is the cafeteria crowded? Engaging the cafeteria staff in conversation is a great way to garner more information about the school's cafeteria and the food. Depending on how your child's school operates and manages the meal service, the lunch ladies may be employed by an outside company and not employed by the school district. Because of the nature of their relationship to the school, it's important to be respectful. Good openers would be: "I just had some questions about school lunch" or "I would like to see the cafeteria." Most people know not to open a conversation with a lunch lady by saying, "What exactly do you feed the kids?" Because some lunch professionals are made to feel defensive about their work, they may hear such questions as criticisms. Most food service personnel at the school level do care about the students' nutrition, but many feel that their hands are tied when it comes to changing menu items; oftentimes they don't have the power to make changes. Many lunch ladies take direction from people in higher positions than at the school level.

When you seek out the lunchroom manager at your school, bring the monthly school lunch menu with you. In some school districts, the school lunch menu is available online if it is not handed out to students on a monthly basis. If you don't have one, ask the lunchroom manager for a menu and ask to discuss it together. He or she should be able to answer your questions about the food. I would start by asking about ingredients in the food items that are served to your child. Does he or she know where to find that information? Starting a respectful dialogue and gauging the opinions and attitudes of the lunch ladies is a necessary step toward establishing a partnership to benefit the students. Another way to develop a positive relationship with the lunch staff is to volunteer your time during lunch. Perhaps you could help serve, restock the salad bar, or help young students manage their food and other related packaging.

Do you know who your child's school nurse is? Many schools don't have the funds to afford a full-time school nurse dedicated to their school. In fact, in Chicago Public Schools, school nurses are spread thin, visiting four or more schools per week. At my large school, even with an enrollment of 1,300 kids, we only have a school nurse on-site for two days each week. If a student comes to the office with a stomachache, fever, or injury on one of the days that the nurse is not on staff, the student is treated by the secretaries in the office.

The nurse at your child's school cares about the health of the students and would be a great person to chat with about school lunches, health, and wellness. Before dropping by to chat with your school nurse, it would be a good idea to call your child's school and make sure that the nurse is on-site before you head over to introduce yourself. Even if the school nurse only spends partial weeks at your child's school, he/she is a powerful ally in the fight for school lunch reform. Nurses have the medical knowledge to fill in the gaps for health and wellness topics.

Any parent is welcome to talk to the school nurse about school health issues. Many schools have health fairs during the school year, and the nurse would most likely be available that day. Additionally, during parent-teacher conferences, nurses are at one of their schools doing paperwork. It's a perfect time to approach the school nurse.

Every school nurse is different. Some may not want to get involved in a committee based in one school if they already have many responsibilities at multiple schools. On the other hand, a school nurse is a powerful connection among many schools throughout the district and could be a vector of information between schools. If you can get a school nurse on your school wellness committee, you'll get a gold star from Mrs. Q. It is invaluable to have a school staff member with medical training on a wellness committee so that he or she can provide the health evidence as proof of the need for change.

Additionally, if your child has a health concern such as allergies or asthma, the nurse is available to help you draft a 504 plan. This is a legal document specifying the accommodations and modifications that a student needs to participate in school. In the case of severe food allergies, there is no need for special education or instruction, but it is best if the school nurse formalizes the paperwork for a 504 that specifies exactly what needs to happen so that the student does not have an allergic reaction to a food at school. If the child needs to have access to an inhaler in order to participate in gym class, access to an EpiPen at school, or needs a peanut-free lunch environment, this can be documented in a 504 plan.

If you have no success with any of the other staff members, approach a special-education teacher, such as a learning disabilities resource teacher, an early childhood special educator, or a speech-language pathologist. Special-education teachers have experience advocating for children with disorders like learning disabilities, vision and hearing problems, and behavioral disorders. Speech pathologists are considered to be special educators because they work with students who have speech disabilities. In general, speech pathologists are unique in that they have the health education and school-based experience that make them sensitive to health and wellness issues in the school environment. Try approaching a speech pathologist or another special-education teacher to see if he or she would be willing to get involved on the school wellness committee. Most "speech teachers" are spread among multiple schools; they might be busy and hard to reach, but it is definitely worth the effort.

Recruiting other parents is a good idea. If there is an active PTA in your child's school, attend a meeting and bring up school lunch. Only you know your own school's PTA. It may already be active in the area of school lunch, or there may not be an active PTA at your school. The PTA is uniquely equipped to help create these bridges between parents and staff in your school. Depending on the culture of your school and your PTA, it may be permissible to create a school wellness committee in collaboration with teachers without going through the PTA. However, depending on the influence of your school's PTA, it may be a better idea to work together to advocate for change.

One caveat: If you are the parent of a teenager, going into the lunchroom to have lunch with your child might be a bad approach. I remember the sheer mortification I felt when my mom came into the school to talk to a teacher. Actually, I had it real bad; my mother was a substitute teacher in the high school I attended. If you are a parent of a teenager, I think it's critical that you get your teenager on board so that you can work together inside the school to make change. Teenagers have opinions and they want to assert themselves and be independent—what better way than to try to change the food system in their small corner of the food world?

Keep in mind that the first thing you are likely to hear is that "there is no money" for reform. As it stands, the National School Lunch Program is underfunded and many school districts and states are grappling with substantial budget deficits that prioritize maintaining teaching positions over procuring salad bars for the cafeterias. However, there are ways to fund school improvements that benefit the health and wellness of students that require only a little creative thinking.

First, seek out partnerships with community organizations that are interested in children's health, including large grocery chains and local hospitals. These organizations may be able to fund the donation of a salad bar or new exercise equipment for the gymnasium. The improvements could be announced at a schoolwide health and wellness fair. In exchange for these donations, the companies would increase their profiles within the community.

Second, research the grants available to schools and start applying. Doing a simple Google search for "educational grants" will yield Web sites that list specific grants for schools based on various criteria (e.g., K–6 school). Additionally, many foundations offer open-ended grants to teachers who write a grant proposal that will enhance learning—and nutrition and physical activity make learning possible.

Last, research local philanthropists to determine their favorite causes. It might be possible that a local resident controls the reins of a family foundation and is interested in children's health and well-being, but is not aware of your school's specific needs. Write a courteous letter introducing yourself and your school and explain what the school needs.

KIDS

Just because you are little doesn't mean that you don't have a say. You are actually eating the food so you have a lot more power than you think. The lunchroom manager and the lunch ladies want your input and your ideas about the food. They care about feeding you and value your opinion. First, tell them your favorite food to eat at school and then tell them your least favorite food. Ask why certain foods are not on the menu. You deserve to know. Ask if there is anything kids can do to change menu items and if there is anything that the students could do to help make lunch ladies' jobs easier.

If you feel that there should be change in the lunchroom, talk to your teachers. Discuss your concerns with them. Ask if a teacher could survey the class for the other students' opinions and if everyone could write a persuasive essay about school lunch.

Additionally, you could run for student council, or if the student council is already formed, you could talk to the teacher who runs the student council about attending a meeting to discuss your concerns with your student representation.

Consider writing a letter to the school district, the food vendor, your representatives (including your state representatives and state senators), and maybe even the president. Never doubt the power of the pen, especially using your voice, the voice of a student who eats school lunch. And guess what? They write back.

Does your class get recess every day? Do you feel like you should be getting more run-around time? I can imagine that the answer is yes. This is an important topic to bring up to your teacher and to your parents. Remind people that recess provides a much-needed physical movement break from sitting down and working.

Talk to your teacher about classroom treats and think about what you would like to do to celebrate holidays and your birthday. Is there a creative way to celebrate that doesn't involve a sugary treat? Maybe your class can do a holiday-themed craft in place of a celebration involving food. Or if food is a part of the holiday, see if the class could write a new nutritious recipe for an old favorite treat.

Consider talking to the lunchroom manager and your teacher about creating healthy-eating posters for the lunchroom to remind students to make responsible choices. If the principal is interested in taking it a step further, see if it would be possible to paint a mural on the walls of the cafeteria of healthful food groups to educate diners and brighten up the space.

TEENAGERS

Your mission, if you choose to accept it, is to make health and wellness "cool." Just saying "health and wellness" makes me want to snore; the phrase is as stale and stuffy as my doctor's waiting room. School lunch reform needs a new marketing and PR department staffed by teenagers. Let's channel some of the time you spend worrying over who's dating whom in a different direction, toward action—changing the food system in your school. Fighting "the man," if you need to think of it that way.

First, I want you to do some critical thinking about your lunch and your cafeteria.

* Does your school have open or closed campus for lunch?

* If there is an open campus, what drives your decision to eat off campus?

* Is eating hot lunch not cool? Is there a stigma around kids eating school lunch at school?

* What do you think about the food in your school?

* Do you pack or do you buy school lunch? Which do you prefer?

* If you like the cafeteria food, what do you like?

* If you don't like the food, what you would like to see changed?

* Have you ever chatted with one of the lunch ladies about lunch?

* Do you think that the cafeteria food is nutritious?

* Do you know if the food is cooked on-site or brought in and reheated?

* If you buy hot lunch, how much do you pay for lunch? Do you think it's a fair price? How does it compare with the cost of a meal you might purchase off campus?

* Do you have a salad bar at your school? What would entice you to eat from the salad bar?

* What's your opinion on fruits and veggies?

* What do you think about fast food?

* What would be your ideal school lunch?

* How do you define health and wellness? Are they the same?

* Are there sufficient opportunities for physical education and/or exercise at school?

If you have concerns about school lunch, would you be willing to approach your teachers and student council members to start a discussion?

Take a picture of your school lunch and share it on social media with your parents' permission. Google "school lunch" to find out how what you eat compares to other students' school lunches.

After you've devoted some time to thinking about school lunch at your school, figure out which of the preceeding questions are the most important for you. For example, if there is a stigma associated with eating school lunch at your school, maybe advocating for the addition of a salad bar would decrease that stigma, increase vegetable consumption, and prevent more kids from leaving campus for fast food.

Start a conversation with the lunchroom manager and find out more information about the lunch served at the school. Find out who provides the food (whether it is brought in by a company or cooked on-site) and ask questions about healthful options offered. Ask if the lunchroom manager has ever surveyed the students to find out which lunch items they prefer and which are their least favorite.

Or if you think that there aren't enough times in the day for students to get exercise, you could suggest a half hour of open gym in the morning before school, opening the weight room to athletes and students before school starts, or inviting a local yoga studio to offer reduced-cost yoga after school once a week.

If you would like to ask around about making change, you may be surprised to find out that other people share your concerns. At my school, the student council brainstormed the things they wanted to change about the school, and right at the top was the quality of school lunches.

Also, you will be doing a little recruiting. Student council already has an "in" with the principal so it would be great if you could get them involved. Or, you might feel more comfortable seeking out the teacher advisor to the student council. You could drop by after school to chat and if you wanted to have a more in-depth conversation, you could make an appointment with the teacher either in person or by dropping a note in the teacher's box.

You could also help form a school wellness committee with parents and teacher support and help plan health and wellness events for your peers to attend and enjoy. If you prefer something less formal than a committee, you and your friends could start a health and nutrition club at your school, or you could start a tradition of packing fun, healthful lunches and enjoying them with your friends (bento lunch boxes are a popular and fun way to inspire you to pack a creative and nutritious lunch; or you could put together a well-planned potluck once a week). However, once your school starts to adopt new, healthful lunch items, be sure to show your support for changes on the menu by purchasing those food items and giving feedback to administrators.

And finally, I don't have to tell you about the power of social networking. Spread the word about school lunch reform and teen nutrition by starting a Facebook page or campaign, and/or tweeting or blogging about the topic.

TEACHERS

School lunch reform is not on the radar of many teachers, as they are not in the cafeteria to see what is being served and they view their lunch period as a break from their students. The ones who are concerned about the school lunch issue may feel helpless because they believe that school lunch is out of the school's control. Since the Department of Education does not manage school lunch or regulate anything that happens in the cafeteria, it's not surprising that many educators don't think too deeply about school lunch reform. However, there are things that teachers can do to create momentum inside individual schools.

First, teachers should start or join a school wellness committee. As I mentioned earlier, a school wellness policy is a district requirement if your school accepts federal funds under the Child Nutrition Act or the Healthy, Hunger-free Kids Act (whose authorization had a rocky path in 2010 but was passed and signed by President Obama in December of 2010). Approach other teachers who have expressed concern about the health and wellness of their students. Creating a committee of teachers in a school is not hard; the hard part is getting things done. Choose one representative to set up a meeting with the principal to inform him or her of the creation of the committee, its purpose, and how it will benefit the school. Hold an informal meeting after school with other teachers and discuss wellness issues (lunch, recess, gym) and the health of the school.

Teachers have a profound impact on their students in many ways, not least as a model for their students. It's more subtle than you think, but students emulate their teachers' food choices, too. Depending on the teacher and the age group, students are interested in knowing everything about their teachers, including their personal food and drink preferences.

Finally, taking control of classroom snacks can have a big impact. How often do you want your students eating cupcakes? Once a month? Consider the number of children's birthdays (twenty to thirty students) as well as classroom celebrations for holidays (Halloween, Thanksgiving, Christmas/Hanukkah, Valentine's Day, St. Patrick's Day, and more—depending on religious and regional celebrations) and it becomes apparent that kids are, on average, eating a sugary snack every other week at school. This is a tough line to walk: Although we don't want to be the cupcake police, we also don't want to jack the kids up on sugar and then try to teach them.

At my school, bringing in sweets for the classroom was a show of status. I found that my students would brag that their parents would be bringing in cupcakes for their birthdays weeks and months before their big day. Yet many kids' parents weren't wealthy enough to buy cupcakes for the whole classroom. If I were a regular classroom teacher, I'd want to tell parents who couldn't afford cupcakes that it's okay to celebrate with a fun craft instead, which could be sponsored by the classroom teacher if necessary. On the other end of the spectrum, if parents are able to afford it, they could provide a small gift for every student instead of cupcakes. Prizes that are popular with my students are cartoon-themed pencils, mini notebooks, fun erasers, stickers, highlighters, and mini picture frames.

If parents insist on sending treats to your classroom, here are some tips you could pass along to encourage healthier snacks for your students:

* Consider offering something that can be consumed by hand without silverware or plates, something simple that can be distributed easily to members of the classroom. Small paper cups can be a great option that eliminates plastic silverware and paper plates.

Cool food ideas include:

* Fill cups with raw veggies (carrots, snap peas, and raw broccoli) or a trail mix with dried fruit.

* Avoid nuts because of the high prevalence of nut-based food allergies, but in their place you could send seeds like sunflower seeds or roasted *pepitas* (pumpkin seeds).

* Make tomato or mango salsa in the classroom and serve with tortilla chips; this way the celebration can turn into a learning event.

* Bring in seasonal fruit like watermelon. (Parents should get an okay from the teacher first due to the mess and need for a knife, but it might be fun for the class to cut up a large watermelon in the early spring or early fall if the student has a summer birthday.)

* Instead of soda pop, send 100 percent juice.

* If your child insists on cupcakes, try sending carrot or zucchini muffins in their place.

But holidays do not need to be celebrated with food. Doing a fun craft, spending time outside, playing a game, or maybe even having a special session with the gym, art, or music teacher would all be wonderful ways to celebrate. A teacher could simply put on some music and throw a fun dance party!

To advocate for bringing back recess, engage the principal on the importance of movement breaks and the fact that many students need to run around before they can organize themselves to participate in and focus on classroom activities. Research has revealed that physical education has a positive influence on concentration, memory, and classroom behavior. The evidence is there—we just need to bring it the appropriate people in power.

CHEFS AND NUTRITIONISTS

Engaging a chef in the school lunch discussion moves the process to a completely different plane. Getting a chef or nutritionist into a school that desperately needs guidance in healthful foods earns you two gold stars from Mrs. Q. The Chefs Move to School program allows chefs to sign up online to be matched with a school that is interested in partnering with a chef.[37] If you have those skills and want to make an alliance with a school that would welcome you, it's a tremendous opportunity for all parties.

However, if you are a parent of a student who attends a local school and you would like to investigate options within your neighborhood, there are ways to open a dialogue with school administrators. A parent/chef/nutritionist would be the perfect person to work with a neighborhood school because I have seen schools respond well to parent stakeholders. If you are a nutrition professional (even if you don't have children), you can still approach a neighborhood school about working with them. Think about these questions to help you develop and refine what you want to accomplish:

* Do you want to lead individual classrooms in preparation of basic foods and basic food education?

* Would you prefer to chat with the principal about working in the cafeteria?

* Do you want to present on a topic during a schoolwide assembly directed toward the student body?

* Do you want to meet the members of the PTA or wellness committee?

* Can you conduct a professional staff development session on healthful classroom snacks on a teacher in-service day or for parents on wellness night?

Many principals offer a variety of assemblies to students, and sometimes it can be a struggle to find and provide diverse presenters year after year. Additionally, the PTA or a local school wellness committee is a good place to introduce yourself to influential members of the community.

First, I would suggest that you do Internet research about the schools in the neighborhood. Using Google, you could find out a lot about the school on the school's Web page, including the names of the key administrators such as the principal. Additionally, you should be able to find out what initiatives the school itself focuses on. Many schools have individualized programs of study and they may already have a school garden or related initiative. Often schools' Web pages have links to information about the PTA and what projects are on the agenda. Then call the school closest to your house to schedule an appointment with the principal or to find out when the next PTA meeting will occur.

You could start a discussion with the principal like this: "Hi, I'm Joe Smith and I'm a professional chef who lives right around the corner from Jones School. I'm interested in visiting the school and presenting a lesson about healthful cooking to the kids. I'd love to set up a time when I can talk to you."

Another way to get a feel for the culture of the school is to attend a PTA meeting. Every school is different and so is every PTA. Some may welcome you and allow you to present your viewpoint right way, whereas other groups may be more hesitant and you might need to attend a series of meetings before you would be able to contribute. In general, PTAs are a great way to connect with people who know the students and understand the community.

EVERYONE HAS A ROLE to help make our schools better. There is a place for all of us—we just have to figure out what our unique talents are and how we can use them to make our country better, one child at a time.

Resources: Organizations

The Center for Ecoliteracy

The David Brower Center
2150 Allston Way, Suite 270
Berkeley, CA 94704-1377
www.ecoliteracy.org
www.facebook.com/centerforecoliteracy
Twitter: @ecoliteracy

For two decades, the Center for Ecoliteracy has been working with schools to create school gardens, to reform school lunch, and to incorporate ecology and sustainability into school curricula. Their Web site offers free downloadable resources including their "Rethinking School Lunch Guide" and "What is a Green School?" to inspire parents and assist reformers. Other helpful materials and services include books, teaching guides, professional development seminars, a sustainability leadership academy, and keynote presentations.

Common Threads

500 N. Dearborn, Suite 530
Chicago, IL 60654
www.commonthreads.org
Twitter: @common__Threads

I was able to volunteer with Common Threads during the summer of 2010 and witnessed firsthand the impact they have on students from low-income households. Through after-school and summer programs, they educate children about nutrition through hands-on cooking classes and working in the garden. In cooking classes, students don't learn how to bake simple cupcakes at Common Threads but instead create soups, entrees, side dishes, and desserts from another part of the world, thereby expanding children's appreciation of global diversity through cooking.

The Edible Schoolyard

Martin Luther King Jr. Middle School

1781 Rose Street

Berkeley, CA 94703

www.edibleschoolyard.org

The Edible Schoolyard, established in 1995, is a one-acre garden and kitchen classroom at Martin Luther King Jr. Middle School in Berkeley, California. It is a program of the Chez Panisse Foundation, a nonprofit organization founded by chef and author Alice Waters. The Edible Schoolyard integrates the classroom, garden, and lunch and is successful because of its devoted community of teachers, students, volunteers, neighbors, and parents. I find the Edible Schoolyard to be a shining example of what is possible when everyone works together.

Farm to School

Occidental College
1600 Campus Road, MS-M1
Los Angeles, CA 90041
www.farmtoschool.org
Twitter: @farmtoschool

Farm to School is a program that connects schools (K through 12) and local farms. The idea is that healthful meals can be served in school cafeterias that improve student nutrition while supporting local agriculture and regional farmers. Each Farm to School program is individualized to its unique community and region as the National Farm to School Network does not impose a list of practices or products for the Farm to School approach. That variability leads to each program meeting the specific needs of the school and its students.

FoodCorps

c/o Wicked Delicate
232 3rd Street, Suite B403
Brooklyn, NY 11215
www.food-corps.org
Twitter: @FoodCorps

A division of AmeriCorps, Food Corps is a recently launched non-profit service organization that is recruiting a crop of young people and recent grads to work a year in school food and school gardens. Food Corps believes that school gardens engage school children so that they learn to make better food choices at school and in their communities. Food Corp members work to establish Farm to School programs and expand nutrition education in schools.

Growing Power
5500 W. Silver Spring Drive
Milwaukee, Wisconsin 53218
www.growingpower.org
Twitter: @growingpower

Growing Power is a national nonprofit organization led by Will Allen, a MacArthur "genius" grant recipient. Mr. Allen's work on his urban farms in Milwaukee and Chicago supports people from diverse backgrounds and the environments in which they live. His powerful voice in urban farming is helping to provide equal access to healthful and affordable food for all people.

Healthy Schools Campaign
175 N. Franklin, Suite 300
Chicago, IL 60606
www.healthyschoolscampaign.org
Twitter: @healthyschools

Healthy Schools Campaign advocates for policies and practices that allow all students, teachers, and staff to learn and work in a healthful school environment. Every spring, the Healthy Schools Campaign hosts a national student chef cooking contest called Cooking up Change. Students from across the country travel to Washington D.C. to compete to create a healthful school lunch within budget. It's empowering for the students and inspirational to nutrition advocates.

The Lunch Box Project

PO Box 20708
Boulder, CO 80308
www.thelunchbox.org
Twitter: @thelunchboxproject

Founded by Chef Ann Cooper, The Lunch Box Project and its nonprofit organization, Food, Family, Farming (F3) Foundation, were created to change the food system in the United States to an ecologically sound, sustainable model. In particular, The Lunch Box Project is an "online toolkit" compiled by Chef Ann to include best practices from around the country to reform school food from highly processed to scratch cooking. Free downloadable tools and resources, including recipes, are available on the Web site. The Lunch Box Project partnered with Whole Foods, United Fresh, and National Fruit and Vegetable Alliance to launch the Great

American Salad Bar Project (Saladbars2schools.org), which was able to raise more than $2 million to date to put salad bars into schools across the United States.

NY Coalition for Healthy School Food

PO Box 6858
Ithaca, NY 14851
www.healthyschoolfood.org
Twitter: @goodschoolfood

The New York Coalition for Healthy School Food is a nonprofit that works to improve the health and well-being of New York's students. Specifically, the New York Coalition for Healthy School Food's goals include incorporating more plant-based foods into school meals, prioritizing local and organic foods where possible, increasing participation in Farm to School programs, creating school gardens, and eliminating competitive foods in the school.

Organic School Project (OSP)

1043 West Grand Avenue
Chicago, IL 60642
www.organicschoolproject.org
Twitter: @organicschool

The Organic School Project works in Chicago with individual schools to convert children into healthy eaters. Their "Grow Teach Feed" model starts by establishing a school garden, then teaching students about healthful living and nutrition, and feeding them cooked-from-scratch food sourced locally.

Physicians Committee for Responsible Medicine: Healthy School Lunches (PCRM)

5100 Wisconsin Ave., N.W., Ste. 400
Washington, DC 20016-4131
(202) 686-2210
www.healthyschoollunches.org
www.facebook.com/PCRMSchoolLunchRevolution

Founded in 1985, PCRM is a nonprofit organization that advocates vegetarian and vegan options be offered to students at school on a daily basis. They believe that plant-based nutrition helps students maintain healthy weights, and they also believe that non-dairy beverage options should be available in the cafeteria due to the high prevalence of lactose intolerance and dairy allergies.

Purple Asparagus

1824 West Newport Ave.
Chicago, IL 60657

www.purpleasparagus.com
Twitter: @PurpleAspChi

Purple Asparagus is a nonprofit organization led by Chef Melissa Graham that is dedicated to teaching kids and families about healthful foods through informal and formal cooking classes and other educational programs across Chicagoland.

Research, Education, Action Policy on Food Group (REAP)
306 E. Wilson St., Suite 2E
Madison, WI 53703
www.reapfoodgroup.org

REAP works to connect producers to consumers, policy makers, educators, and businesses so that the links between land and eating are meaningful. REAP is committed to projects that sustain family farmers and encourage ecological-friendly agricultural practices.

School Food FOCUS
c/o Public Health Solutions
40 Worth Street, 5th Floor
New York, NY 10013
www.schoolfoodfocus.org
Twitter: @schoolfoodfocus

School Food FOCUS is a national initiative that supports large school districts with enrollments of forty thousand or more students that want to change their school food systems and obtain more healthful and locally-sourced food. FOCUS was named a 2010 Top Nonprofit by Philanthropedia.

School Lunch Initiative
www.schoollunchinitiative.org

The School Lunch Initiative was formed in 2004 as a public-private partnership among the Chez Panisse Foundation, the Center for Ecoliteracy, and the Berkeley Unified School District to research and quantify the experiential learning in instructional gardens, kitchen classrooms, and school classrooms. A report of the findings of their September 2010 study can be found on their Web site.

School Nutrition Association
120 Waterfront Street, Suite 300
National Harbor, MD 20745
www.schoolnutrition.org
Twitter: @schoollunch

The School Nutrition Association is a national, nonprofit industry organization that is the face of more than fifty thousand school nutritional professionals.

- - - - - - - - - -

Veggiecation
PO Box 5121
Ridgewood, NJ 07451
www.veggiecation.com
Twitter: @veggiecation

Founded by Titanium Spork Winner Lisa Suriano, the Veggiecation Program is a curriculum-based lunch program that introduces young children to vegetables as many children have limited exposure. Veggiecation curricula is incorporated into the classroom education and the school lunch programs.

Resources: Food Blogs

- - - - - - - - - -

Better DC School Food
Betterdcschoolfood.blogspot.com

The official blog of Parents for Better D.C. School Food, this site is managed by Ed Bruske, who also blogs at TheSlowCook.com. The cornerstone of the group's advocacy is replacing highly processed, sugary food with wholesome, nutritious food in District of Columbia public schools.

- - - - - - - - - -

Better School Food

Betterschoolfood.org

Founded by long-time school food reformer Dr. Susan Rubin, Better School Food is a group of dedicated parents, educators, and health professionals committed to improving school meals and increasing awareness of the connection between good food and effective learning.

Brave New Lunch

Bravenewlunch.blogspot.com

The blog discusses the challenges, issues, and ideas surrounding improving the quality and nutrition of school food. Ali declares that she is "the next generation of lunch lady: college educated, professional chef, and on a mission to change school lunch."

Food Politics

www.foodpolitics.com

Food Politics is written by Marion Nestle, a leading nutrition expert and professor at New York University. She covers a wide variety of topics related to our food system, including school food.

Jackie's School Food Blog (United Kingdom)

Jackiesschoolfoodblog.blogspot.com

Labeled the "Mrs. Q of England," in 2005, Jackie successfully organized a group of parents, created an organization, and changed school meals in her hometown of Merton.

The Lunch Tray

www.thelunchtray.com

The Lunch Tray is a daily blog written by Bettina Elias Siegel devoted to "kids and food, in school and out." Updated several times a day, five days a week, the blog features breaking news items, essays, and guest blog posts on a wide variety of topics relating to children and food (everything from picky eaters, to treats in school, to childhood obesity), with a special emphasis on school food reform.

New Haven School Food: Notes from Chef Tim

www.nhschoolfood.blogspot.com

Chef Timothy Cipriano is the executive director of Food Services for New Haven Public Schools and blogs about his mission: to ensure that delicious, healthful meals are available to all New Haven students. Chef Tim was one of only two chefs selected by President Obama to attend the Childhood Obesity Summit at the White House in April 2010. On his blog, Chef Tim shares his insights and experiences with school food.

Parents, Educators, and Advocates Connection to Healthy School Food (PEACHSF)

Peachsf.org

Headed up by Titanium Spork Winner Dana Woldow, this coalition of parents, teachers, and concerned community members turned around the San Francisco School District's school food through persistence and cooperation. The frequently updated "How-to Guides" lay out practical plans for collaboration with school staff and district administration to achieve common goals.

What's Cooking with Kids

Whatscookingwithkids.com

What's Cooking is a Certified Green business led by Michelle Stern that offers healthful and seasonal cooking classes to children of all ages in the San Francisco Bay Area. Michelle also works to improve the school lunch program in local schools.

Resources: Helpful Links

- - - - - - - - - -

Jamie Oliver's Food Revolution

www.jamieoliver.com/foundation/jamies-food-revolution

Coming off of the Emmy Award–winning television show *Jamie Oliver's Food Revolution*, Jamie has continued his mission to change the way people eat for the better. Through his Web site, Jamie continues to educate his passionate following about food and cooking and to encourage parents to find out what their children are eating at school.

- - - - - - - - - -

Let's Move!

www.letsmove.gov/healthierschoolfood.php

The goal of the Let's Move! campaign, started by First Lady Michelle Obama, is to solve the challenge of childhood obesity within a generation. The online presence of Let's Move! creates a community around wellness and offers simple tools to help kids and families be more active, eat better, and get healthy.

- - - - - - - - - -

United States Department of Agriculture — National School Lunch Program (NSLP)

www.fns.usda.gov/cnd/Lunch

The National School Lunch Program (NSLP) was established by President Harry Truman in 1946. The program funds low-cost or free lunches to children, depending on the income of their parents, who attend public school or nonprofit private schools. The lunches provided must meet federal nutrition guidelines to qualify for reimbursement.

Resources: Further Reading

Edible Schoolyard: A Universal Idea by Alice Waters (2008). The history of the garden and cooking transformation of one amazing school in Berkeley, California.

Food Politics: How the Food Industry Influences Nutrition and Health by Marion Nestle (2007). A well-researched look into the governmental policies driving food consumption and food advertising in our country.

Free for All: Fixing School Food in America by Janet Poppendieck (2010). A lengthy discussion about the current state of the National School Lunch Program, its history, processed foods offered to students, and why the program should be free for all students.

Lunch Lessons: Changing the Way We Feed Our Children by Ann Cooper and Lisa Holmes (2006). Written from a chef's point of view, the book conveys the serious problems with eating processed foods daily and the importance of cooking with fresh foods. The book features recipes for parents to make for their children's lunches.

Omnivore's Dilemma: A Natural History of Four Meals by Michael Pollan (2007). Tracing the food Americans eat from table back to its source, Pollan describes the industrial food complex with astounding detail.

School Lunch Politics: The Surprising History of America's Favorite Welfare Program by Susan Levine (2008). A historical text about the National School Lunch Program. A great exploration of the politics and culture of food and the challenges the program has faced over the years.

End Notes

Chapter 1

1. J. L. Brown and E. Pollitt, "Malnutrition, Poverty, and Intellectual Development," *Scientific American* 274:2 (1996): 38–43.

2. Center on Hunger, Poverty, and Nutrition Policy, *Statement on the Link between Nutrition and Cognitive Development in Children* (Medford, MA: Tufts University School of Nutrition, 1995).

3. For the definition of food deserts: www.cdc.gov/Features/FoodDeserts.

4. Share Our Strength's report on hunger: Shareourstrength.org/school_breakfast/pdfs/report_full.pdf.

5. National School Lunch Program, Facts Sheet, www.fns.usda.gov/cnd/lunch/aboutlunch/NSLPFactSheet.pdf.

Chapter 2

6. Chicken nuggets contain less that 50 percent chicken. See Michael Pollan, *The Omnivore's Dilemma: A Natural History of Four Meals* (New York and London: Penguin Press, 2006).

7. Ingredients in a Chicken McNugget: Nutrition.mcdonalds.com/nutritionexchange/ingredientslist.pdf.

8. Twenty-nine million pounds of antibiotics were given to U.S. livestock in 2009. See www.fda.gov/downloads/AnimalVeterinary/GuidanceComplianceEnforcement/GuidanceforIndustry/UCM216936.pdf.

9. A picture of mechanically separated chicken: www.fooducate.com/blog/2009/08/03/guess-whats-in-the-picture-foodlike-substance.

10. Bisphenol A (BPA) is in the lining of canned foods. See "As BPA Concerns Rise, Can Companies Seek Alternatives," News .discovery.com/human/bpa-canned-foods-alternatives.html.

Chapter 3

11. Lunch lady shares that school pizza has sixty-two ingredients: Fedupwithschoollunch.blogspot.com/2010/03/guest-blogger-pizza-perspectives.html. See also Bravenewlunch.blogspot.com.

12. The USDA's National School Lunch Program Web site is www .fns.usda.gov/cnd/lunch.

13. E-mail conversation with Lisa Suriano from Veggiecation about pizza and grains, January 14, 2011.

Chapter 6

14. Obesity data gathered from the Centers for Disease Control: www.cdc.gov/obesity/data/trends.html; www.cdc.gov/obesity/data/index.html.

15. The Childhood Obesity Report released by the White House in May 2010: www.aap.org/obesity/pdf/tfco_fullreport_may2010.pdf.

Chapter 7

16. The federal reimbursement rate for school lunch: www.fns .usda.gov/cnd/governance/notices/naps/nsl10-11t.pdf.

17. Chicago Public Schools Press Release: www.cps.edu/About_CPS/The_Board_of_Education/Documents/BoardActions/2010_04/10-0428-PR9.pdf.

18. Robert Wood Johnson report on competitive foods: www .calendow.org/uploadedFiles/competitive_foods_brief.pdf.

Chapter 8

19. R. Barros, E. Silver, and R. Stein, "School Recess and Group Classroom Behavior," *Pediatrics* 123:2 (February 2009): 431–36.

20. Historical information about the elimination of recess: Ceep.crc.uiuc.edu/poptopics/recess.html.

21. W. Strong, et al, "Evidence Based Physical Activity for School-age Youth," *Journal of Pediatrics* 146 (2005):732–37, www.healthywv.com/shared/content/page_objects/content_objects/pdf_documents/youth_pa_recs.pdf.

22. H. Taras, "Physical Activity and Student Performance at School," *Journal of School Health* 75:6 (August 2005): 214–18.

Chapter 9

23. The Summer Food Service Program Web Site is www.summerfood.usda.gov.

24. Michael Pollan, *The Omnivore's Dilemma: A Natural History of Four Meals* (New York and London: Penguin Press, 2006).

Chapter 10

25. Margot Sanger-Katz, "Smart Food," Boston.com, February 27, 2011, www.boston.com/lifestyle/health/articles/2011/02/27/smart_food/?page=full.

Chapter 11

26. "A Sweet Problem: Princeton Researchers Find that High-fructose Corn Syrup Prompts Considerably More Weight Gain," www.princeton.edu/main/news/archive/S26/91/22K07.

27. Article reporting that chocolate milk contains three teaspoons of added sugar: "School District Says 'No More Chocolate

Milk,'" www.thedenverchannel.com/news/21983366/detail.html. Mayo clinic's information on high-fructose corn syrup: www.mayo clinic.com/health/high-fructose-corn-syrup/AN01588.

28. The dairy industry's opinion on flavored milk: www.milk delivers.org/schools/flavored-milk.

Chapter 12

29. Research on the effects of Jamie Oliver's menu changes on school performance: Institute for Social and Economic Research, "Jamie's Dinners Add up to Better Results for Pupils," www.iser .essex.ac.uk/news/2009/02/02/jamies-dinners-add-up-to-better-results-for-pupils.

30. National School Lunch Program, Facts Sheet, www.fns.usda .gov/cnd/lunch/aboutlunch/NSLPFactSheet.pdf.

Chapter 13

31. Great school lunches are available in Marblehead, Massachusetts at the Marblehead Community Charter School where chef Laura DeSantis, Titanium Spork Winner, works (Marbleheadcharter .org/foodservice). Other inspiring examples are the Academy for Global Citizenship in Chicago, Illinois; Boulder School District's lunches under the leadership of Ann Cooper; San Marco Unified School District's Wellness Policy (www.smusd.org/wellnesspolicy); and San Francisco Unified School District's Wellness Policy (www .sfusdfood.org/pdfs/SFUSDWellness.pdf.) For further amazing school lunches, check out "School Meals That Rock!" on Facebook.

32. The Academy for Global Citizenship's lunches are provided through Chartwells, and Namaste Charter School's lunches are provided through Sodexo.

33. Janet Poppendieck, *Free For All: Fixing School Food in America* (Berkeley: University of California Press, 2010).

34. Dr. Susan Rubin's Web site is www.drsusanrubin.com/blog.

35. Chef Ann Cooper's Let's Move Salad Bars 2 Schools Web site is Saladbars2schools.org.

36. Jamie Oliver's Food Revolution, www.jamieoliver.com/foundation/jamies-food-revolution/home.

Mrs. Q's Guide to Quiet Revolution

37. Chefs Move to Schools Sign-up Form: Healthymeals.nal.usda.gov/schoolmeals/Chef/ChefsForm.php.

Acknowledgments

Thank you to the small group of people who kept my secret. It's official—you can now talk freely! I couldn't have done this without the support of my family. My husband, Mike, watched Charlie so I could spend weekends at our local library writing the book without the distractions of rambunctious toddler behavior, the laundry, and dishes. To my wonderful mother, Mary, thank you for driving down from Wisconsin with dinner every other weekend so that I could return from the library to a hot meal and, most important, your smile. And thanks to Holly, my sister, and Peter, my father, who supported me from afar with their frequent phone calls and e-mails.

To my friends and family who sustained me from near and far, including every single Burns, Roth, and Wu—thank you! Friends who have been encouraging during the writing process—Allison Stark, Viveka Neveln, Adam Metz, Megan Kennelly, Caroline Hanson, Danna Olsen, Elaine Wu, Siris Rivas, Victoria Margolin, Zachary Crain-Davis, Colleen Harrah, Amanda Dowd, Donna Caranto, Andrew Burns, Luc Di Gregorio, Natalee Aiello, Leslie Bauer, and anyone I forgot to mention. May everyone be as lucky as I am to call you friends.

To Andy Bellatti for first noticing the blog on Twitter—I owe you.

I would like to thank my blog readers for their devotion to the project and input along the way. To all of the people in the school food reform movement and fellow food bloggers who supported me through phone calls and e-mails. Thanks go to Dr. Susan Rubin, Ed Bruske, Michelle Stern, Dana Woldow, Lisa Suriano, Alison St. Sure, Kim Foster, Andrew Wilder, Sarah Henry, Mud Baron, Sarah Elizabeth Ippel, Robyn O'Brien, Bettina Elias Siegel, Marion Nestle, Mark Bittman, Shauna James Ahern, Melissa Graham, Jamie Oliver, Chef Ann Cooper, and all of my fabulous guest bloggers.

I'd like to thank my agent, Sarah Bridgins, who e-mailed me with the question, "Have you considered turning your project into a book?" Sarah, you are simply the best. I owe a huge sum of gratitude to my freelance editor Judy Sternlight, whose guidance was invaluable.

A big thanks to my editor, Leigh Haber, for connecting with Fed Up With Lunch and seeing its importance in the larger discussion of food politics. To Laura Lee Mattingly, Doug Ogan, Claire Fletcher, Jennifer Tolo Pierce, Steve Kim, and Lorraine Woodcheke at Chronicle Books, thank you so much for your hard work on *Fed Up with Lunch*.

I would like to thank Chicago Public Schools for giving me the opportunity to work with hundreds of terrific students and families. I love being a speech-language pathologist for CPS. To all the students, teachers, and staff of Haugan Elementary School, I want to tell you it has been a pleasure working with you all. I want to thank "Pearl" and her excellent lunch staff for feeding 1,300 students every day and me for one year. Thank you for working so hard to feed hungry children.

Index

- - - - - - - - - -

About the Author

Sarah Burns Wu is a speech-language pathologist working in the Chicago area. "Mrs. Q" has been interviewed on *Good Morning America*, National Public Radio, and the *Gayle King Radio Show*. Fed Up With Lunch: The School Lunch Project has been featured on Yahoo!, MSNBC.com, CNN.com, ABCNews.com, and AOL Health, and in *USA Today*. Originally from Wisconsin, Wu moved to Chicago in 1999 after graduating from the University of Wisconsin-Madison with a BA in Spanish to work for Kraft Foods. After four years at Kraft, she changed careers hoping to make a difference in the lives of children. In 2006, Wu completed an MA in speech-language pathology from Northwestern University. She is the married mother of a toddler and lives and teaches in Illinois. She continues to blog at FedUpWithLunch.com—it remains a gathering place for people concerned about children's food and health. Her Twitter handle is @fedupwithlunch.